FLAT EARTH: SATAN'S GLOBAL PLAN OF DECEPTION

HELIOCENTRISM EXPOSED

CASPIAN "CASPER" SARGINSON, J.D.

SARGINSON PUBLISHING

CONTENTS

SATAN STANDS ON THE PRECIPICE OF DOOM

PREFACE

I believe that Satan's entire master deception since the beginning of time rides on his success of keeping the truth about his heliocentric lie hidden from you and the rest of the world. I believe that exposing the lie and the sorcery of heliocentrism and revealing the truth about God's creation of the Earth is likely to be the beginning of a worldwide spiritual awakening, like the reformation of Martin Luther's time.

I certainly hope so, and I pray for revival driven by a renewed passion for the Word of God—Sola Scriptura!

Now you know why I wrote this book.

WHEN DECEPTION IS EXPOSED
TRUTH IS REVEALED

A 5,000 piece jigsaw puzzle would be extremely difficult to assemble, and that assumes you had a copy of the final image on the box to use as a guide. If, however, you didn't have an image of the finished product, but thousands of little Polaroid snapshots of various related activities and people to look at before you started to work on the puzzle, it would be an extraordinary challenge. That challenge would become insurmountable if the majority of those Polaroid images were of dubious clarity, some hazy, others torn and missing sections, and some almost entirely faded. Trying to put together Satan's comprehensive plans on this Earth are even more difficult. If we cannot envision his overall goal and strategies, we cannot recognize the context of deceptions that come our way. This book will assemble enough, but not all, of the pieces of Satan's massive deception so you will begin to see the full scope of his deception in all its glory, and so you can see where his heliocentric deception fits on the giant puzzle. May God open your eyes as he sees fit.

CHAPTER 1
WHAT MAGIC TRICK?
SORCERY ON A SCALE THAT'S HARD TO BELIEVE

The entire world has been fooled as if a magic trick was performed before every living soul. The magic has been so powerful, it spans centuries and continents, and no one has been beyond the reach of its spell.

The greatest sorcery of our time is denied with expressions like these:

How could they fool the whole world? How could they possibly deceive me my whole life? How could they keep a secret like this so long? How many people would have to be part of the lie, and how could all those people keep the secret? The science is proven. Everyone knows the Earth is not flat.

Is flat Earth just conspiracy talk, or has Satan pulled off the biggest scam in the history of the world? After extensive research into both the Bible and "real science," including a review of the theology and science of many brilliant scholars throughout history, and having exposed multiple lies and frauds, I have concluded as a trained lawyer that the evidence is overwhelming, and the verdict must be that Satan did, in fact, pull off the biggest deception, not just of our time, but of all time.

The big mystery that has confronted all of us in this age is how could he possibly have done it? How could Satan have fooled nearly the entire world? How could we as Americans be so thoroughly and adamantly convinced the Earth rotates around an axis at 1,037 mph at the equator, revolves around the sun at 66,600 mph, while simultaneously the sun (and the Earth and the planets) revolve around the center of the "solar system"[1] at 500,000 mph, all while the "solar system" is carried by our galaxy at 1.3 million mph through the Universe.

How could Satan possibly convince us that the Earth is a globe, that it curves around a tight radius of 3,959 miles, and that our eyes are lying to us when we see nothing but flat horizons across the oceans and from 30,000 feet?

If it is true that the firmament contains Earth's space in a contained system, and it is impossible to fly through the firmament into a vacuum called "outer space," how in the world could NASA have created such convincing photos and videos and massive programs that get televised live for us to watch?

So convincing has Satan's master plan been, we have not only been persuaded to believe, we adamantly believe. We will fight anyone who opposes the heliocentric model, and even the words "flat Earth" are fighting words.

This doesn't feel like the kind of deception we've experienced many times in our lives. This feels like such a fantastical magic trick that it cannot possibly be imagined, not on this scale!

Christians have not been exempt from this sorcery. They are as convinced as everyone else that the Earth is everything Copernicus and NASA have claimed.

The greatest magic trick is the one you never saw. It's the trick you think didn't happened. It's the magic you missed and as you look at the landscape, all you see is ordinary life. This is often when you hear the magician say, "Move along folks. There's nothing to see here."

In the chapters to follow, I will for the first time connect all the dots throughout history so you can see how all this happened and how we got to this place of massive deception so big, we can't even believe it ourselves.

I will take many pieces of the massive puzzle that have laid in disarray for centuries, and put enough of the pieces together so you can begin to see the formation of an image, a master plan that was implemented long ago.

Are you ready? I hope you are capable of setting aside the powerful defensive forces within your flesh known as cynicism and pride, because if you are not humble and teachable in a biblical sense, you cannot see what God is revealing to many of us in this great awakening that is happening around the world today.

We speak wisdom, however, among them that are full grown: yet a wisdom not of this world, nor of the rulers of this world, who are coming to nought: but we speak God's wisdom in a mystery, even the wisdom that hath been hidden, which God foreordained before the worlds unto our glory: which none of the rulers of this world hath known: for had they known it, they would not have crucified the Lord of glory: but as it is written, "Things which eye saw not, and ear heard not, And which entered not into the heart of man, Whatsoever things God prepared for them that love him." 1 Corinthians 2:6-9

If we are to understand the greatest magic trick ever performed, we must understand the bigger picture. We need to comprehend the master plan and how the master sorcerer sets the stage if we are to have the capacity to see through the present deceptions.

In Chapter 2, *What is the Master Plan?*, we examine

Satan's number one purpose since he came on stage. In Chapter 3, *Satan's Strategies*, we review his major strategies in order to recognize his methods. In Chapter 4, *Satan's Effort to Keep The Word of God From Us*, we see his extraordinary effort to keep us in the dark. Black magic is most successful in fooling its victims when darkness hides the truth.

Once having laid the foundation upon which heliocentric sorcery is built, the rest of the book unpacks the evil at work, ultimately exposing the magician's tricks for all to see, and relying upon the Word of God for a full revelation of the truth.

---

1. "Solar system" is in quotes in this book, because there is no "solar system." The Bible's full description of God's creation of the "heaven and earth" does not include anything like a "solar system," nor does the Bible mention anything like "outer-space." Chapter 8 explains in detail God's precise description of the Earth, the open expanse above us, and the solid firmament over the Earth. The sun and the moon are "in the firmament" according to Genesis, and the stars and planets are also within or below the firmament. The sun is not the center of a "solar system," and the Earth and planets and asteroids and comets do not revolve around the sun. There is no "solar system."

CHAPTER 2

WHAT IS SATAN'S MASTER PLAN?

ONE RING TO RULE THEM ALL

The War of the Ages between Satan and God has raged for thousands of years. Satan has a powerful evil and well organized army, and guess how Satan learned to organize his forces? He learned from none other than the greatest and wisest of all commanders while he was still Lucifer in Heaven. Lucifer observed how God organized all the Angels and heavenly hosts, and as Satan does with everything else, he simply tried to copy what God does.

Do not think for a moment that Satan simply shoots from the hip, and conducts his warfare with random commands to demons who have not been prepared to play their role in this war.

Satan has revealed his master plan many times, and understanding that master plan will help us immensely to put more of the pieces of the puzzle into their proper place.

Among all Satan's evil schemes, what single goal rules them all? What one goal of Satan is above all other goals and plans and is the focus of his most intense passions?

Satan's Evil is Displayed For All to See

You could justifiably argue that his biggest evil scheme is Darwinian evolution, the idea that man came from primordial soup, crawled from the sea onto land, and evolved into a monkey and eventually into a stunning model walking a runway in New York.

That is an evil scheme, one that has far reaching implications for the human race, our identity, our purpose, and the beliefs that mold society and life as we know it. It certainly has eternal consequences for the souls who reject God as our Creator and Savior.

You could argue that the international multi-billion dollar human trafficking and pedophilia industry is the biggest evil covered up today by all kinds of chicanery. It truly is evil beyond comprehension. Why don't "they" stop such horrendous crimes? Those who have the power to stop sex trafficking are the very people who profit by it. This is part of the deception that is far worse than most people ever comprehend.

Depending on your political persuasion, you might feel that corruption within the American government involves layers of deception that are so deep and wide, even within national security agencies, that the citizens will never know how deep that rabbit hole goes. You would be right.

Many have argued that main street media is part of a massive deceptive network of propaganda, coordinated with politicians and big tech that seeks to control the entire world's communications in pursuit of their goal of a global government, and they would be right about that.

Some have devoted their lives to exposing the deception of Hollywood, the music industry, and the other entertainment industries, and how they are polluting the minds of our children. God bless those who fight to expose deception everywhere, but like the other deceptions, these are just one small section of the greater puzzle.

Others will point to the weaponization of our health care system, to the corruption of big pharma, and the power of the government to shut down the entire country. Such powerful deception has dramatically increased in recent years, especially since the pandemic.

Then we have the curriculums developed in universities and our Department of Education that have turned our education system into a mass propaganda program for all kinds of evil. The implications last for generations.

Perhaps one of Satan's biggest deceptions are the many false religions of the world. The most prominent of all religions throughout history involved in deception is unquestionably the Roman Catholic Church. In fact, the Roman Catholic Church plays such a major role on Earth facilitating Satan's master plan, we will come back to this at the end of Chapter 4.

Satan's Master Plan Unmasked

We will unmask Satan's master plan, and you'll see it is much bigger than all of these evil schemes and deceptions, bigger even than all the false religions of the world combined. It is the master plan that rules them all.

Satan's master plan is the guiding force that rules all of Satan's strategies and tactics, including all of his deceptions.

The master plan to rule them all can be expressed this way:

> Satan's master plan from the first time his scheme revealed itself in the Garden of Eden was and has continued to be throughout history, among people in every nation and every age, to turn people away from God, to diminish God in their eyes, to persuade them they don't need God, but ulti-mately to convince all people that there is no God. At the same time, like a double-edged strategy that has both a direct result and a consequential result, Satan has sought to convince the world he doesn't exist either. The genius in this scheme is that the spiritual default for the human race falls to worldly living and worshipping anyone but God.

This may sound obvious to you, and you may say, "Well, I already knew that!" Knowing his master plan is good, but the applications of his master plan as a guiding force that determines his strategies and tactics used to develop grand deceptions against the human race is where the magic begins.

If everyone understood these things, they would not constantly question why evil events happen, why people commit egregious crimes, how it is that politicians make the decisions they do, why and how false flag events happen resulting in the rapid deprivation of our freedoms, including religious freedom, and they would not live in such confusion over how all the deceptions and evil of today fit together in the bigger picture. People would not be so easily fooled by Satan's sorcery.

Sorcery is effective only when its victims are ignorant of the ways of Satan, and when they do not know the Word of God.

BELIEVERS HAVE GROSSLY UNDERESTIMATED SATAN'S DECEPTION

The reason christians don't comprehend the power and depth and breadth of Satan's deception is because they have grossly underestimated it.

Satan is not just after your body or your soul, and he's not just after control of the entire world. You and I, and even all the treasures of this Earth are not the big prize. The real prize for Satan is the entire human race!

SATAN'S MASTER PLAN REVEALED IN HISTORY

Satan's master plan has revealed itself many times in history, but if you don't know what to look for, you'll miss it. The phrase, "War of the Ages" is an excellent description of this war between Satan and God. On either side are the two smartest military commanders in the heavens and on earth. Let's be clear, Satan doesn't compare to God, but apart from God, there is no other angel who was above Lucifer in Heaven, and there is no man on earth more knowledgeable than Satan.

Satan's plan to destroy the human race, including all believers, starting with God's chosen people, the Jews and the nation Israel, nearly succeeded, or so Satan thought. Satan was close to a major victory of snatching the entire human race out of God's hands. Genesis tells us the story:

> Now it came about, when mankind began to
> multiply on the face of the land, and daughters
> were born to them, that the sons of God saw that
> the daughters of mankind were beautiful; and they
> took wives for themselves, whomever they chose.
> Then the LORD said, "My Spirit will not remain
> with man forever, because he is also flesh; never-
> theless his days shall be 120 years." The Nephilim
> were on the earth in those days, and also afterward,
> when the sons of God came in to the daughters of
> mankind, and they bore children to them. Those
> were the mighty men who were of old, men of
> renown. Then the LORD saw that the wickedness of
> mankind was great on the earth, and that every

intent of the thoughts of their hearts was only evil continually. Genesis 6:1-5

Satan spent thousands of years on his plan to destroy the human race, to pollute its DNA, and in particular to make sure there would be no pure blood line from Eve to the eventual mother of Jesus Christ, The Savior of the world.

Recall the punishment God issued to Satan after the fall of Adam and Eve as a result of Satan's temptation and deceit. God said to the Serpent Satan:

And I will put enmity between thee and the woman, and between thy seed and her seed; it shall bruise thy head, and thou shalt bruise his heel. Genesis 3:15

We all know Adam and Eve's blood line led all the way to the baby Jesus, but what is this about Satan having a blood line? Some theologians argue that when God used the words "thy seed" to Satan, he was referring to all human beings who would live and die without Christ. In other words, God meant that in a symbolic sense to refer to those in sin, essentially that Satan is the father of all sinners.

That meaning can easily apply to anyone who lives in sin and dies without Christ. That's an obvious meaning, but where scripture can be taken literally, we have to be very careful deciding ourselves that God didn't mean it literally. In other words, you have to have a very good reason not to take a verse literally in the Bible before you attribute a metaphorical or other figurative meaning to it.

THE SEED OF SATAN

In this case, we don't have to speculate, because Genesis 6 tells us what the seed of Satan refers to. In Genesis 6:1-5 we have a clear narrative. We are told that when man was populating the earth, the "sons of God" saw that "the daughters of mankind were beautiful; and they took wives for themselves, whomever they chose."

The "sons of God" were fallen angels, and that is clearly documented in Appendix C if you want the biblical proof. The Nephilim were the offspring of the union between fallen angels and the daughters of men. If you doubt that, you will see ample biblical proof in Appendix C. You'll also see that the "mighty men" referred to as the Nephilim, were also giants.

The biblical proofs involve many verses, the Hebrew and Greek original meanings of the words used, the context, the genealogies in the Old Testament making it clear who is the line of Jesus and who are the lines leading to the rebellious evil blood lines, and the connected Bible stories. If you're going to understand the truth of these issues from the Word of God, it's going to require that you do the diligent studies necessary. I've done much of that work for you in Appendix C.

CONNECTING THE DOTS

Immediately after Genesis 6 describes the sin of the fallen angels and the growing population of the giants or Nephilim, what is next? Let me show you:

The Nephilim were on the earth in those days, and also afterward, when the sons of God came in to the daughters of man and they bore children to them. These were the mighty men who were of old, the men of renown. The LORD saw that the wickedness of man was great in the earth, and that every intention of the thoughts of his heart was only evil continually. Genesis 6:4-5

The egregious sin by the Nephilim is immediately followed by the connection to the evil in the hearts of ALL men on the earth (except Noah and his family). The point is made again a few verses later:

Now the earth was corrupt in God's sight, and the earth was filled with violence. And God saw the earth, and behold, it was corrupt, for all flesh had corrupted their way on the earth. And God said to Noah, "I have determined to make an end of all flesh, for the earth is filled with violence through them. Behold, I will destroy them with the earth. Genesis 6:11-13

Notice that "all flesh had corrupted their way on the earth." How do you suppose that happened? The chronological sequence of these verses in Genesis clearly connects this sin and the fact that "the earth is filled with violence" with the activity of the fallen angels and their offspring, the Nephilim, and the fact that the Nephilim were populating the earth and corrupting it. They were corrupting it in every way, through violence and sin of every kind, and by polluting the human race with their DNA.

Remember these were offspring of fallen angels. These were evil angels, often called demons. Satan was trying to fill the earth with his DNA, his evil blood line, in the hopes of polluting the pure blood line that he knew was required for the future Savior of the world, who had to be perfect.

GOD FLOODED THE EARTH AND KILLED THEM ALL

Satan's plan did not succeed, because God flooded the entire earth and drowned every human being on earth, including all the Nephilim and all their offspring. Noah and his wife and their three sons were the only Godly people left on earth whose blood had not also been corrupted by fallen angels' heirs. I address the three wives of Noah's sons in Appendix C, if you want to pursue that.

I'm not suggesting that man was not responsible for his own sin, and that all sin should be blamed on the Nephilim or on Satan. Don't even go there, because that certainly is not my argument. When Adam and Eve fell to sin in the Garden of Eden, sin entered the human race.

From that point everyone born would be born in sin and in need of a Savior. While Satan was the tempter and instigator in the Garden of Eden, and continues in that capacity, fallen man's destiny is not dependent on Satan or his demons.

The point of the Genesis 6 story about the flood and it's cause tells us much about Satan's efforts to destroy the human race and "get back at God" for casting him out of Heaven and condemning Satan. Satan is the father of lies, the great deceiver, and he has been working to destroy all of God's chosen people, including you and me.

Let there be no doubt that Satan seeks your misery, your destruction, and if possible, your soul's eternal condemnation.

> Be sober, be vigilant; because your adversary the
> devil, as a roaring lion, walketh about, seeking
> whom he may devour. 1 Peter 5:8

Satan worked for thousands of years to corrupt mankind, to drive people away from the Living God into occult worship, and to humiliate God's human creation in front of God for all to see in the heavens and on the Earth.

And then in one powerful demonstration of God's mighty wrath, which the Angels, good and bad, had never seen before and did not know God was capable of, God ended that era with the worldwide flood, killing all of Satan's wicked servants, all of the giants or Nephilim, and God restarted the world and the human race.

Here We Are Again

We are now living in a time that has a prophetic similarity to the days of Noah just before the flood! God makes a connection between the sin of Noah's time and the sin of the last days before he saves all his chosen ones.

After Jesus had described the coming of the end times, he was asked by his disciples, ***"Tell us, when will these things happen, and what will be the sign of Your coming, and of the end of the age?"*** Matthew 24:3

Jesus' answer was epic:

> For the coming of the Son of Man will be just like
> the days of Noah. For as in those days before the
> flood they were eating and drinking, marrying and
> giving in marriage, until the day that Noah entered
> the ark, and they did not understand until the flood
> came and took them all away; so will the coming of
> the Son of Man be. Matthew 24:37-39

After the Earth was repopulated, it didn't take long for Satan to rebuild his evil empire, and he did so first with the Babylonian Empire. Nimrod was the first king after the flood, and he was an evil king who claimed to be a god, demanded the people worship him, and he was a tyrannical ruler known to be a hunter of animals and men.

Nimrod was determined to build his kingdom, and he decided to build a tower to Heaven, later to become known as the Tower of Babel.

The Tower of Babel was no myth, and it was not a sham either. We know this because it is recorded as true history in the Bible, and we know this because just before God stopped Nimrod's assault, God said "now nothing will be restrained from them, which they have imagined to do," meaning they were about to be able to accomplish anything they could imagine, which in context indicates there was more to the Tower of Babel than most of us have thought.

> And they said, Go to, let us build us a city and a tower, whose top may reach unto heaven; and let us make us a name, lest we be scattered abroad upon the face of the whole Earth. And the LORD came down to see the city and the tower, which the children of men builded. And the LORD said, Behold, the people is one, and they have all one language; and this they begin to do: and now nothing will be restrained from them, which they have imagined to do. Genesis 11:4-6

There are other extra-biblical historical sources known as apocrypha, indicating that Nimrod intended to enter Heaven and assault God and his angels. Some have suggested that Nimrod was Satan, and others suggest Nimrod is at least a type of Satan. We really don't need extra-biblical sources to tell us that Nimrod's intent was evil if he was trying to build a tower to reach Heaven. It certainly wasn't to hold a birthday party for Jesus. Like Satan, Nimrod was evil to the core.

God destroyed the Tower of Babel, and divided the people into many language groups and spread them throughout the world. This was ground zero for all the religions of the world today.

SATAN TRIES AGAIN

Millennia have passed again, and Satan's plan to take down the entire human race has taken a different course this time. Jesus knew the course Satan would take, because Jesus warned us three times in Matthew 24 of the "deception" to come.

Deception comes in many colors, so when describing Satan's deception, we can't assume all deception is of the same kind or identifying the same event. There is general deception, specific deception, minor deception, major deception, deception that causes no consequential harm, and deception that has massive eternal consequences. Jesus specifically warned of deception in the last days, and he mentioned false teachers who would lead people astray, but in 2 Thessalonians 2:11 we are told about "a strong delusion," referring to a single major deception that God will send to the earth.

> Therefore God sends them a strong delusion, so
> that they may believe what is false, in order that all
> may be condemned who did not believe the truth

but had pleasure in unrighteousness. 2 Thessalonians 2:11-12

Satan's deception regarding the heliocentric system is not the delusion of 2 Thessalonians, but it certainly is one of the biggest, if not the biggest deception of Satan's post-flood career. It has consisted of thousands of little deceptions, many major deceptions, and it has involved propaganda and lies and pseudoscience and millions of participants over the years. We are now approaching the fulfillment of his deception, which seeks to bring mankind once again to the brink of total destruction.

Only when Satan believes that he has captured the entire human race and kept as many souls as possible outside the saving grace of Jesus Christ, does Satan picture himself once again trying to assault the Heavens to complete his original goal of defeating God and ruling Heaven and Earth.

There is some debate about Satan's ultimate goal with God, whether it is to "be like God," or defeat God and take his throne. That debate comes out of these verses:

> *How art thou fallen from heaven, O Lucifer, son*
> *of the morning!*
> *How art thou cut down to the ground, which*
> *didst weaken the nations!*
> *For thou hast said in thine heart, I will ascend*
> *into heaven,*
> *I will exalt my throne above the stars of God:*

I will sit also upon the mount of the congrega-
tion, in the sides of the north:
I will ascend above the heights of the clouds; I
will be like the most High. Isaiah 14:12-14

I understand the argument that the last verse says, I will be like the most High," but the previous verses strongly indicate that Satan wants to replace God. He wants to exalt his throne "above the stars of God." Since the stars as described in Genesis are below or in the firmament, and since we are also told God's throne sits on top of the firmament, Satan was saying his throne will be where God's throne is. No one would imagine two thrones in Heaven side by side with God on one and Satan on the other. I'm certain that is not Satan's vision either. Satan wants to be like God, but he also wants to replace God. They cannot both rule the heavens and the Earth.

God cast Lucifer out of Heaven along with the Angels under Lucifer's command, and so ended Lucifer's first assault on the Kingdom of God. But it would not be his last.

People often wonder how one-third of the Angels in Heaven could possibly decide to rebel against God and join Satan in the rebellion. That seems absolutely insane. The scriptures do not tell us, but I would propose that a third of the Angels were under Lucifer's command in Heaven, and he ordered them to follow him. There was and is a chain of command in Heaven, and if it is anything like the chain of command in our own military branches, a soldier must obey his commander's orders.

The next grand assault on Heaven would be the Tower of Babel. Following that, Satan tried to assault Heaven again by trying to get Jesus to join him in his rebellion against God by tempting him, and when that didn't work, Satan tried a direct final assault through the Son of God, one member of the Trinity, by killing Jesus on a cross.

Little did Satan anticipate that this very assault on the Trinity, the crucifixion of the Savior of mankind, Jesus Christ, would result in the salvation of all whom Satan had tried to steal from God, and would result in the victory that would ultimately bind Satan for 1,000 years when Jesus himself comes in wrath to judge Satan, and that it would lead to the end for Satan at the Great White Throne Judgment when Satan is once and for all cast forever into the Lake of Fire.

We know the victory has already been won through Christ. As Jesus said on the cross, "It is done!" But Satan is not one to surrender. He is cruel. He is a liar. He is a deceiver, a murderer, and the most evil creature to ever have existed. So he plots and schemes, and he makes his war plans, and he plans his deceptions.

What are we to do in defense? How are we to handle ourselves in times like these? The Bible tells us:

Take heed that no man deceive you. For many shall come in my name, saying, I am Christ; and shall deceive many. And ye shall hear of wars and rumors of wars: see that ye be not troubled: for all these things must come to pass, but the end is not yet.

For nation shall rise against nation, and kingdom against kingdom: and there shall be famines, and pestilences, and earthquakes, in divers places. All these are the beginning of sorrows. Then shall they deliver you up to be afflicted, and shall kill you: and ye shall be hated of all nations for my name's sake. And then shall many be offended, and shall betray one another, and shall hate one another. And many false prophets shall rise, and shall deceive many. And because iniquity shall abound, the love of many shall wax cold. But he that shall endure unto the end, the same shall be saved. And this gospel of the kingdom shall be preached in all the world for a witness unto all nations; and then shall the end come. Matthew 24:4-14

And we are told to conduct ourselves as soldiers for Christ by putting on the defenses God gives us:

Finally, my brethren, be strong in the Lord, and in the power of his might. Put on the whole armor of God, that ye may be able to stand against the wiles of the devil. For we wrestle not against flesh and blood, but against principalities, against powers, against the rulers of the darkness of this world, against spiritual wickedness in high places. Wherefore take unto you the whole armour of God, that ye may be able to withstand in the evil day, and having done all, to stand. Stand therefore, having your loins girt about with truth, and having on the breastplate of righteousness; And your feet shod with the preparation of the gospel of peace; Above all, taking the shield of faith, wherewith ye shall be able to quench all the fiery darts of the wicked. And take the helmet of salvation, and the sword of the Spirit, which is the word of God: Praying always with all prayer and supplication in the Spirit, and watching thereunto with all perseverance and supplication for all saints. Ephesians 6:10-18

Clearly, we are to be thinking christians who know our enemy, and who properly use weapons of war for offense and defense. This book is intended to help you do exactly that.

In the following chapters we begin to assemble the pieces of the grand evil puzzle, the individual deceptions that are a part of the massive deception that is the guiding force at play today.

WE ARE EASILY DECEIVED
MEDITATE ON THIS

"We think far too little of God's majesty and
   power,
and not enough of Satan's deceptions." Casper
   Sarginson

CHAPTER 3
SATAN'S STRATEGIES
STRATEGIES, DECEPTIONS, & MASS FORMATION

S atan has many strategies and tactics that he uses again and again throughout the ages. It is helpful to recognize them as we fit ourselves for the whole armor of God.

Satan twists the Word of God. In fact twisting the Word of God was Satan's first magic trick in the Garden of Eden when he tempted Eve and misquoted God, and further twisted what God said by telling Eve if she ate of the fruit of the Tree of Knowledge of Good and Evil, she would know what God knows.

Satan twisted God's Word when he tempted Jesus three times. Though Satan quoted the scriptures correctly, he misapplied them in tempting Jesus.

We need to know the Word of God ourselves and not be dependent on others who may twist God's Word for their own purposes. Every single christian should know how to study and interpret the bible using fundamental principles of interpretation found in hermeneutics and exegesis.

Be diligent to present yourself approved to God as a worker who does not need to be ashamed, accurately handling the word of truth. 2 Timothy 2:15

And while you're learning, be careful who you choose to teach and mentor you. There are many wolves in sheep's clothing.

<u>Satan disguises himself</u>:

2 Corinthians 11:13-15 For such men are false apostles, deceitful workmen, disguising themselves as apostles of Christ. 14 And no wonder, for even Satan disguises himself as an angel of light. 15 So it is no surprise if his servants, also, disguise themselves as servants of righteousness. Their end will correspond to their deeds.

Christians need to develop discernment to recognize deceivers. Too many christians are far too trusting and gullible and believe everything they are told by authority figures.

Beloved, do not believe every spirit, but test the spirits to see whether they are from God, because many false prophets have gone out into the world. 1 John 4:1

Satan imitates God. The apostles encountered a demon possessed man by the name of Simon (Acts 8:9-24). He was known for practicing sorcery for a long time. When he offered to pay Peter for the power of the Holy Spirit, Peter rebuked him. Simon wanted to imitate true believers.

In the last days during the tribulation, the Beast and the False Prophet will perform great signs and wonders imitating Jesus and God's servants. (Revelation 13:13; 16:14; 19:20) It's amazing how many christians today are taken in by preachers performing great signs in what is often called the "health and wealth gospel."

Satan counterfeits God. Satan tried to counterfeit God's knowledge and wisdom in the Garden of Eden. He counterfeited God's Kingship and power repeatedly as the god of this world, working through Emperors, Pharaohs, Kings, and Queens.

Satan attempted to counterfeit God's pure genetic line from Noah to Seth to Abraham to Isaac to Jacob and all the way to Jesus when the other fallen angels mated with women on Earth as described in Genesis 6.

Satan counterfeited God as the Angel of Light, and has many names: Accuser, Adversary, Angel of Light, Angel of the bottomless pit, Antichrist, Beast, Beelzebub, Belial, Deceiver, Devil, Dragon, Enemy, Evil One, Father of Lies, King of the Bottomless Pit, Lawless One, Leviathan, Liar, Lucifer, Murderer, Power of Darkness, Prince of the Power of the Air, Ruler of the Darkness, Ruler of this World, Serpent of Old, Son of Perdition, Fallen Star, Tempter, Thief, and Wicked One.

Satan counterfeits God's Temples with his own satanic temples, and he creates millions of gods for people of many religions to worship.

Satan counterfeits the gift of tongues first witnessed on the Day of Pentecost with false demonstrations of speaking in tongues today. Satan also counterfeits healings and miracles with sorcery and magic.

Satan will also counterfeit the Holy Trinity in the later half of the 7-year tribulation with himself as a god figure, the Beast as the Son of God, and the False Witness as the Holy Spirit. The Beast even comes back from the dead (or nearly dead) again to imitate Jesus.

Satan kills, steals, destroys. He's been doing this for as long as we've had recorded human history. He is ruthless, heartless, narcissistic to the extreme and psychotic, seeks death and destruction wherever he goes, hates with an intensity we cannot begin to comprehend, and he does seek whom he may devour.

Satan afflicts and oppresses. Demons afflicted many with diseases and created mental strife as well as recorded in Luke 13:16, and Jesus drove out demons in Matthew 8:16. Demon possession has been displayed around the world, and mental disease is seen in masses of people who are tortured mentally and psychologically.

Satan falsely accuses. Satan is the accuser and slanderer of God's people, and we saw that when Satan entered God's presence to accuse Job of being a faithless believer, and falsely claiming that the only reason Job was faithful was because God had blessed him with great wealth. (Job 1:6-11)

How many people has Satan made to feel worthless, depressed, desperate, and suicidal? Millions upon millions. Satan blinds and confuses:

2 Corinthians 4:3-4 And even if our gospel is veiled, it is veiled to those who are perishing. 4 In their case the god of this world has blinded the minds of the unbelievers, to keep them from seeing the light of the gospel of the glory of Christ, who is the image of God.

Spiritual matters are spiritually discerned:

1 Corinthians 2:14 The natural person does not accept the things of the Spirit of God, for they are folly to him, and he is not able to understand them because they are spiritually discerned.

Satan distracts and hinders. The Apostle Paul said Satan hindered him from getting to Thessalonica, and Jesus indicated Satan hindered a conversation he was having with Peter in Matthew 16:21-23.

Satan is the Father of Lies. Why would christians assume that governments and political organizations and corporations all are altruistic and behave just like Jesus would on all matters for all of time?

You might say, "No, christians don't assume those

things," to which I would say, "They surely do. They believe everything NASA says about the creation of the earth and the heliocentric system."

All of this is the fertile soil upon which Satan designed the heliocentric system of occult worship. People are only too easily deceived.

CHAPTER 4

SATAN'S EFFORT TO KEEP THE WORD OF GOD FROM US

AND IN THE ALTERNATIVE TO KEEP US FROM KNOWING IT AND BELIEVING IT.

S atan's theme underlies all his deceptions, all his sorcery, all of his magic tricks. He is the father of lies, and everything he schemes, facilitates, coordinates, masterminds, and does is founded upon lies. If Satan's fingers have touched it, it is corrupt.

Throughout history Satan has worked on this Earth through people and human organizations, at least in our visible world. In this chapter I will assemble many pieces of the puzzle revealing who those people were, what organizations they used, and most importantly how their accomplishments were designed to fit perfectly into Satan's master plan of deception from the beginning of time.

My hope is that this will act as a catalyst to clear whatever fog may remain in your mind about Satan's master plan of deception, and specifically so that you will begin to see clearly how Satan has been trying to keep God's true creation story from you.

If your eyes are open to how the scriptures actually describe God's creation of the Earth, and you begin to recognize Satan's grand sorcery of the heliocentric system through pseudoscience and scientism, Satan's entire master plan of deception since the Garden of Eden collapses, and that means it loses its power over you forever.

THE MASSIVE DECEPTION THAT TRIGGERS SPIRITUAL REVIVAL

I believe that Satan's entire master deception since the beginning of time rides on his success of keeping the truth about his heliocentric lie hidden from you and the rest of the world. I believe that exposing the lie and the sorcery of heliocentrism and revealing the truth about God's creation of the Earth is likely to be the beginning of a worldwide spiritual awakening, like the reformation of Martin Luther's time.

In the 16th century when Martin Luther posted his 95 Thesis on the door of his church in Wittenberg, he exposed the deception and lies of the Roman Catholic Church, and you could say, "All hell broke lose."

It was the catalyst for a worldwide reformation and brought to the fore Satan's plans to keep all people from God. Luther exposed the practice in the Roman Catholic Church of selling indulgences, denying the scriptures in the most fundamental of doctrines, including salvation through Jesus Christ, and the authority of the scriptures.

The Roman Catholic Church did all it could in its power to keep the Word of God, the Bible, from falling into the hands of the ordinary person, or anyone outside the ranks of the Catholic priesthood. The Vatican prohibited any English translations of the Bible, and actively sought to keep the Bible from the people for over 1,000 years.

As a result of the reformation and courageous christians of the 16th century, the Bible did get translated into English, and the KJV of 1611 was published. It is the single biggest selling book in all of world history. Most people don't realize how big a loss the publication of the KJV was for Satan. The last thing Satan wants is for all people to have access to God's Word.

The battle to keep the Word of God from all of mankind lasted for thousands of years, and guess who headed that effort up for Satan on Earth? It was the Roman Catholic Church. Keeping the Bible from the people became the passion and a primary goal of the Papacy. This is all well documented in treatises and hundreds of books and commentaries. In this book, we need to stay focused on the big picture and not get derailed by trying to convince the in-convincible.

The Vatican was so determined to stop anyone from translating the Bible into the layman's language, they destroyed every early effort to translate any part of the Bible, they burned Bibles that had been translated, and the Vatican persecuted and put to death those who did translate the Bible. Here's a brief history of the Roman Catholic Church's war to keep God's Word and truths away from all of us.

You'll see how important the Roman Catholic Church's role has been in promoting this heliocentric plan from hell. Not only did the Pope endorse Copernicus' heliocentric model in 1533, 10 years before Copernicus published his book, but the Church also fought to keep the Bible out of the hands of the common man. If Satan can keep the people ignorant of God's Word, he can convince them of anything, especially if they are willing to "follow the science.

There is a tremendous volume of history throughout the centuries that prove beyond a shadow of a doubt that the Roman Catholic Church was heavily invested in keeping the Bible from the layperson, and laying down the law that only the Roman Catholic Church could understand the Bible. But let's get to the point much faster by simply quoting the Church's own dogma.

Decree of the Council of Toulouse (1229 A.D.): "We prohibit also that the laity should be permitted to have the books of the Old or New Testament; but we most *strictly forbid their having any translation of these books."*

Ruling of the Council of Tarragona of 1234 A.D.:
"No one may possess the books of the Old and New Testaments in the Romance language, and if anyone possesses them he must turn them over to the local bishop within eight days after promulgation of this decree, so that they may be burned..."

Proclamations at the Ecumenical Council of Constance in 1415 C.E.: *Oxford professor, and theologian John Wycliffe, was the first (1380 A.D.) to translate the New Testament into English to "...helpeth Christian men to study the Gospel in that tongue in which they know best Christ's sentence." For this "heresy" Wycliffe was posthumously condemned by Arundel, the archbishop of Canterbury. By the Council's decree "Wycliffe's bones were exhumed and publicly burned and the ashes were thrown into the Swift River."*

Fate of William Tyndale in 1536 A.D.: *William Tyndale was burned at the stake for translating the Bible into English. According to Tyndale, the Church forbid owning or reading the Bible to control and restrict the teachings and to enhance their own power and importance.*

There is much more to be known about the true history

of the Roman Catholic Church, far more than we can cover here. I have included the best documentary I have found on the full explanation of the Church's involvement in heretical doctrines of demons and their shameful and shocking history in Appendix D: The Deception of the Roman Catholic Church.

If you understand the history of the Roman Catholic Church, you'll have a much deeper understanding of how we have been deceived today, and how so many people continue to miss the plain meaning of the scriptures. Deception is most effective with those who do not know the scriptures, and therefore have no defenses and little spiritual truth upon which to base their beliefs.

CATHOLICS TODAY DO NOT KNOW THE BIBLE

Even today, 500 years after the violence of the 16th century reformation and the publication of the KJV in 1611 and many English versions since then, Catholics do not know the Bible. The Roman Catholic Church actively keeps people out of the Bible. How do they do that when they claim the Bible is their authority? They do it with great deception, and here's how.

The Catholic Church teaches that the Bible is one of three equal authorities for Catholics. The other two that are said to be equal to the Bible are Catholic Church tradition and the authority of the Catholic Bishops (the Magisterium). In actual practice, tradition and the Bishops are above the Bible. In public they say the Bible is equal, but that's not what they practice. It is part of their grand deception to keep people from the truth of the Word of God, which if people truly knew, would cause them to see all the heresy in the Catholic Church.

The Catholic Church today plays a continuing role in Satan's master plan and the deceptions he is using to blind as many as possible. Let's run through a quick chronological history.

The Pope was briefed by his personal secretary on the heliocentric system in 1533, and he immediately adopted it as the Catholic Church position.

It was a Catholic Cardinal who persuaded Nicholas Copernicus to write and publish his theory of heliocentrism. Here is the main part of that letter:

Rome, 1 November 1536
Nicholas von Schonberg, Cardinal of Capua to Nicolaus Copernicus,
Greetings.
. . . I had learned that you had not merely mastered the discoveries of the ancient astronomers uncommonly well but had also formulated a new cosmology. In it you maintain that the earth moves; that the sun occupies the lowest, and thus the central, place in the universe . . .
Therefore with the utmost earnestness, I

entreat you, most learned sir, unless I inconvenience you, to communicate this discovery of yours to scholars.

Farewell

It has been said by other historians that Copernicus only wrote and published his book, *On The Revolutions of The Heavenly Spheres*, after the Catholic Church's persuasion. Copernicus was, after all, a canon (a church administrative role that at the time required ordination to minor orders) at his uncle's diocese in Warmia. He held a doctorate in canon law. Clearly Copernicus was deeply steeped in the doctrine and traditions of Catholicism.

With Cardinal Wolsey in the lead, the Catholic Church created a new approach to defeat those who opposed the heliocentric view. Who opposed the heliocentric system? Almost everyone outside the Catholic Church, including the entire Protestant church, Martin Luther, John Calvin, and essentially all the non-Catholic church leaders of the time.

Woolsey's new approach was diabolical and has become the mainstay for all argumentation to support heliocentrism and fight the biblical view of a flat Earth. He called his approach, "Learning against learning," and by it he meant to set up a learned approach to be administered by Catholic supporters who could intellectually argue with a new set of data and knowledge called science. Of course, it was really lies and pseudoscience, but Woolsey's approach was a phenomenal success. It is even today, the most successful approach in support of heliocentrism.

Woolsey created the first encyclopedia in history, which of course, was part of the "learning against learning" that would promote the lies and pseudoscience to help the Catholic Church fulfill its perceived mission to keep the common citizens in darkness.

CATHOLIC DOCTRINE IS ANYTHING BUT BIBLICAL

If you grew up a "good Catholic," and you later were saved by faith in Christ alone, then you would know about these egregious heresies and anti-biblical teachings of the Catholic Church:

- The Jesus Christ of the Catholic Church is not the same Jesus Christ of the Bible,
- That you are not saved in the Catholic Church by faith "in Christ alone," but by continuing works,
- That you are specifically saved only when you receive water baptism in a Catholic baptism,
- That you can lose your salvation in the Catholic Church,
- That it is mandatory that you attend Catholic masses and take communion so you can be forgiven for the sins you committed throughout the week,

- That when a Priest blesses the bread and the wine in communion, the Priest calls Jesus down from Heaven to be sacrificed again literally, and that the bread becomes the actual real body of Christ, and the wine becomes the actual real blood of Christ, which is called Transubstantiation,
- That Catholic Priests can pray for someone who died without being saved by Christ and who is in a fictitious place called Purgatory and save their soul,
- That Jesus' mother, Mary was perfect and saved herself and that Catholics can receive forgiveness for their sins through Mary,
- That the Bishops of the Catholic Church and the Pope are infallible,
- And the list of heresies and anti-Christ beliefs and practices go on and on.

The Roman Catholic Church is so deceptive that virtually no Catholics in good standing understand how all of these doctrines and practices are anti-biblical and that the "good Catholic" who believes and practices all of these things—according to the Bible—is definitely not saved by faith in Christ alone.[1] Catholics genuinely have no idea they have been so thoroughly deceived. This kind of mass deception for centuries over the whole world reminds me of the mass deception for centuries over the whole world on heliocentrism.

Here's a point of interest for those of you who study human behavior and how the mind works. You will be especially interested in how people could be so thoroughly deceived, and still be adamant about staying in those beliefs even when they are provably wrong. Those who have been completely immersed their whole lives in the Roman Catholic Church display exactly the same mental, emotional, psychological, and spiritual defenses as do those who have been deceived to believe the earth is a globe that revolves around the sun. The defensive profile is identical. And both are typically absolutely adamant, and refuse to study the proof that they are wrong. This is the power that being deceived can wield over a person and their eternal soul. Unless they are set free in Christ and no longer blinded, they will remain in bondage. If you'd like to pursue this further, I recommend a book entitled, Destroying Strongholds of the Mind: The Battlefield of the Real War.

It may be helpful to know that both God and Satan blind people which keeps them in bondage. Here are the two verses that tell us this:

SATAN BLINDS PEOPLE.

And even if our gospel is veiled, it is veiled to those who are perishing. In their case the

god of this world has blinded the minds of
the unbelievers, to keep them from seeing
the light of the gospel of the glory of Christ,
who is the image of God. 2 Corinthians 4:3-
4

GOD BLINDS PEOPLE.

Though he had done so many signs before them,
they still did not believe in him, so that the
word spoken by the prophet Isaiah might be
fulfilled:
"Lord, who has believed what he heard from us,
and to whom has the arm of the Lord been
revealed?"
Therefore they could not believe. For again
Isaiah said, "He has blinded their eyes and
hardened their heart, lest they see with
their eyes, and understand with their heart,
and turn, and I would heal them." John
12:37-40

The Apostle Paul put together some of the pieces of the
puzzle for us in what I like to think of as reverse engineering.
Sometimes we see something bizarre, and we don't know how
it came to be, but if we can reverse engineer it by unraveling the
mess to understand how it could have happened, we can see
the original cause and the sequence that led to the final result.

Paul did that in Romans, showing us how people's sin and pride and obstinance lead to bondage and to God turning them over to a depraved mind. Here are those verses, and while this is a long quote from Romans, it is critical that we follow Paul's line of thought all the way through. Notice the incredible relevance of Pauls' words, not only for the blindness that comes from the deception and sin, but because Paul specifically mentions God's creation. Wow! This could not be more on point! These verses are from Romans 1:18-32.

For the wrath of God is revealed from heaven
against all ungodliness and unrighteousness of
men, who by their unrighteousness suppress the
truth.
For what can be known about God is plain to them,
because God has shown it to them.
For his invisible attributes, namely, his eternal
power and divine nature, have been clearly
perceived, <u>ever since the creation of the world</u>, in
the things that have been made. So they are
without excuse.
For although they knew God, they did not honor
him as God or give thanks to him, but they became
futile in their thinking, and their foolish hearts
were darkened.
Claiming to be wise, they became fools,
and exchanged the glory of the immortal God for

images resembling mortal man and birds and animals and creeping things.

Therefore God gave them up in the lusts of their hearts to impurity, to the dishonoring of their bodies among themselves, because they exchanged the truth about God for a lie and worshiped and served the creature rather than the Creator, who is blessed forever! Amen.

For this reason God gave them up to dishonorable passions. For their women exchanged natural relations for those that are contrary to nature; and the men likewise gave up natural relations with women and were consumed with passion for one another, men committing shameless acts with men and receiving in themselves the due penalty for their error.

And since they did not see fit to acknowledge God, God gave them up to a debased mind to do what ought not to be done.

They were filled with all manner of unrighteousness, evil, covetousness, malice. They are full of envy, murder, strife, deceit, maliciousness. They are gossips, slanderers, haters of God, insolent, haughty, boastful, inventors of evil, disobedient to parents, foolish, faithless, heartless, ruthless. Though they know God's righteous decree that those who practice such things deserve to die, they not only do them but give approval to those who practice them.

These verses hit all the preconditions that lead to depravity and blindness:

1. Men suppress the truth by their unrighteousness;
2. Since the <u>creation of the world</u> God's invisible attributes are made known to all men (this refers to God's true creation, not the heliocentric counterfeit);
3. And they are left without any excuse;
4. They exchanged the glory of the immortal God for images resembling mortal man and birds and animals and creeping things (all of which is represented in all its glory in the gods and images associated with the planets, the sun, and the heliocentric design);
5. All of which leads to all sins God hates;
6. And since they would not acknowledge God, he gave them over to a debased mind ("depraved mind" in the NASB and "reprobate mind" in the KJV);
7. Which then leads into further sin, including a long list of repulsive sins that will bring God's wrath in the end.

The Roman Catholic Church has been the chief of coverups, false pretenses, misrepresentations, fraud and deception. Even their own Priests, Bishops, Archbishops, and Cardinals and not likely to be christians because they deny Christ and the fundamental tenets of the faith. One could not possibly survive within that anti-Christ environment if you were a genuine christian. That would be like asking the Apostle Paul to consider Hell his home and safe haven. It could not be.

The Roman Catholic Church is the biggest cult the world has ever known, and they play a major role in promoting the heliocentric sorcery of Satan today. I strongly recommend you watch the video in Appendix D.

THE VATICAN OPERATES
THE MOST POWERFUL TELESCOPE ON EARTH

What is the Vatican doing in space exploration? Do they really own a large telescope in Arizona?

"The Mount Graham International Observatory (MGIO), operated by Steward Observatory, is the research arm for the Department of Astronomy at The University of Arizona. MGIO consists of three telescopes: the Vatican Advanced Technology Telescope, the Heinrich Hertz Submillimeter (Radio) Telescope of the Arizona Radio Observatory, and the **Large Binocular Telescope**, the **world's most powerful telescope**." Source: Mount Graham International Observatory, Arizona State Website, 2023.

The "Large Binocular Telescope" is also known as LBT,

but it has a much longer acronym, LUCIFER. This is not a joke. LUCIFER happens to stand for "Large Binocular Telescope Near-infrared Utility with Camera and Integral Field Unit for Extragalactic Research." Need some proof of that?

"We know that the Vatican telescope is known as the VATT so what is the Lucifer telescope and where did it come from? L.U.C.I.F.E.R stands for Large Binocular Telescope Near-infrared Utility with Camera and Integral Field Unit for Extragalactic Research (bit of a mouthful). This tool is very powerful and allows astronomers to see incredibly distant objects in the universe. Using infrared technology this tool has lead to amazing discoveries about the formation of stars and planets and has massive potential for even more discoveries about and distant planets." Source: The Vatican Owns And Operates a "Lucifer Telescope" But Why?, UFOHOLIC, 2023.

The Vatican actually has a large organization that manages their Mount Graham telescope, and guess who manages it? The Jesuits. We're not going to open another can of worms for the Catholic Church, except to say that the Jesuits have a rich history going back to the days of the 16th century enforcing the Vatican's tyranny. The man who founded the Jesuits under the Pope's direction was Ignatius Loyola. Loyola was an avid proponent of using education to create obedient minds.

"Ignatius Loyola demanded obedience of the understanding. An obedient understanding alters its perception of reality according to the superior's dictates, 'We must hold fast to the following principle: What seems to me white, I will believe black if the hierarchical Church so defines.'" Source: F. Tupper Saussy, Rulers of Evil, page 47.

Here's a description of the Vatican organization operating the telescope:

> The <u>Vatican Advanced Technology Telescope</u> (VATT) is located on Mt. Graham in south eastern Arizona, and is part of the Mount Graham International Observatory. The Vatican Observatory Research Group (VORG) operates the 1.8m Alice P. Lennon Telescope with its Thomas J. Bannan Astrophysics Facility, known together as the Vatican Advanced Technology Telescope.

The Vatican does own the most powerful telescope on Earth, and the Vatican uses the research and the studies from that telescope to support and promote the continuing hoax that we live in a heliocentric system.

Do you still think the Catholic Church is a christian church?

---

1. Catholics or people who used to be Catholic have a very hard time with these biblical truths. For example, one man who was raised in a Catholic Church told me that he was taught as a youth that their saving faith is in Christ, and to him that meant Catholics are saved.

What he wasn't told was that the Church doctrine did not actually state that Catholics are saved by faith in Christ alone. Instead, they are saved in a Catholic baptism, and Priests can absolve them of sin, that Priests can save them after they died and went to Purgatory, that Mary offers them salvation because she lived a perfect life, and that the Bible is only one of three Church authorities, with the other two being Church tradition and the infallible Bishops and Pope. Where the Bible contradicts tradition, tradition rules. Where the Bible contradicts infallible Bishops or the Pope, the Bible loses. But the deception lies in keeping all this from good Catholics. These things are never explained with the Bible. The Catholic Church does not teach directly from the Bible using reliable methods of hermeneutics and exegesis. Instead the Priests teach tradition and Catholic dogma. The Jesus of the Roman Catholic Church is not the Jesus of the Bible.

CHAPTER 5

HELIOCENTRISM: THE PREEMINENT SYMBOL OF ANCIENT OCCULTISM

EARTH AND PLANETS BOW DOWN TO THE SUN GOD

D id you know the entire heliocentric system of a spherical Earth rotating and revolving around the sun with other planets was actually designed after ancient occultic beliefs?

The heliocentric system is not real. It never was, but its imaginary design fulfills Satan's grand purpose of misdirecting the human race away from the True Creator God.

It's an endlessly complex design that fills the time and energy of millions of people who grew up playing with toy space shuttle's and imagining what it would be like to become astronauts and explore far away planets and galaxies.

As adults, millions have become fixated on all things NASA. They watch every new video, gape over every new CGI (computer generated image), hang on every word of scientists who wax eloquent with fantastical pseudoscientific theories.

The elaborate scheme constructed over centuries, launched officially with Copernicus' book in 1543, has been Satan's single greatest act of sorcery and occult magic on Earth. It achieved the grand success he pursued to turn billions of souls away from any recognition or acknowledgement of a God of Creation.

Satan's sorcery has accomplished something few are aware of, even theologians and pastors, and something that Satan fully intended in the heliocentric design. What is this purpose that drives Satan's hatred and passion?

The heliocentric design of the sun and the Earth and the planets mocks God. It mocks God as the Creator of the "heaven and the Earth." It mocks God by appropriating his Glory in creation. It mocks God by counterfeiting God's own creation story. It mocks God with false gods. And the heliocentric system mocks God by trying to expunge the entire history of God's miraculous works on Earth, but most importantly it mocks God with the claim that there never was a savior, Jesus Christ.

If you ever thought as a christian that the controversy of whether the Earth is flat or a sphere is not important, think again. God does not consider mocking his holy character or denying him the glory that is due him as an insignificant matter.

Considering how God values his glory, to mock him so boldly in front of the entire human race, to mock God to all the angels of Heaven, and to mock God to all the fallen angels who can see, is a reminder to the genuine believer of what this means to a Holy God whose wrath is coming against all ungodliness.

> See that no one deceives you with empty words, for because of these things the wrath of God comes upon the sons of disobedience. Therefore do not become partners with them; for you were once darkness, but now you are light in the Lord; walk as children of light (for the fruit of the light consists in all goodness, righteousness, and truth), as you try to learn what is pleasing to the Lord. Do not participate in the useless deeds of darkness, but instead even expose them; for it is disgraceful even to speak of the things which are done by them in secret. But all things become visible when they are exposed by the light, for everything that becomes visible is light. For this reason it says, "Awake, sleeper, And arise from the dead, And Christ will shine on you." Ephesians 5:6-14

It's truly amazing how occult sorcery put such evil plans out in the open, yet we all have missed the obvious. This is the magician distracting his audience from God's reality and deceiving all the spectators into believing a false reality. What is so extraordinary is that this heliocentric sorcery is on a grand scale, and yet we still missed the obvious.

Do you know why it has not even occurred to pastors and theologians that the heliocentric system mocks God? Because they have been ensnared by Satan's sorcery like everyone else. They think heliocentrism is real, and therefore the thought that it mocks God never enters their minds.

Let's look at the obvious we all have missed for so long.

HELIO-SORCERY: A MODEL OF OCCULT WORSHIP

In Greek mythology, the sun god was one of their primary gods. Their sun god was Helios which is how they named the heliocentric system. Heliocentrism is designed with the sun at the center with lesser bodies, like the Earth and the planets, revolving around the sun symbolic of worshipping the sun god.

The sun is not a minor fixture within this larger architectural design. It plays a major role in the symbolism of the heliocentric system. The sun had a major focus for the ancients in Rome, Greece, Egypt, and throughout the ancient empires.

Sun worship was prevalent in ancient Egyptian religion, and the earliest deities associated with the Sun are all goddesses: Wadjet, Sekhmet, Hathor, Nut, Bast, Bat, and Menhit.

From at least the 4th Dynasty of ancient Egypt, the Sun was worshiped as the deity Ra. In the Middle Kingdom of

Egypt, Ra lost some of his preeminence to Osiris, lord of the West, and judge of the dead.

The Sun's movement across the sky represented a struggle between the Pharaoh's soul and an avatar of Osiris. Ra travels across the sky in his solar-boat; at dawn he drives away the demon king Apep. The "solarization" of several local gods (Hnum-Re, Min-Re, Amon-Re) reached its peak in the period of the fifth dynasty.

In Aztec mythology, *Tonatiuh* was the sun god. In Incan mythology Inti is the ancient Incan sun god. In Irish mythology the sun god is *Grian*. The Deity of the Sun in Chinese mythology is Ri Gong Tai Yang Xing Jun (Tai Yang Gong/Grandfather Sun) or Star Lord of the Solar Palace, Lord of the Sun. In Germanic mythology, the sun is personified by Sol.

In Greek mythology, Helios, a Titan, was the personification of the Sun. The Ancient Greeks also associated the Sun with Apollo, the god of enlightenment. The heliocentric system is named in honor of Helios.

Even in Nicholas Copernicus' own famous introduction of the heliocentric system in his book, *On The Revolutions of The Heavenly Spheres*, published in 1543, he revealed his own occultic worship of the sun with this statement on page 151:

> "At rest, however, in the middle of everything is the
> sun. For in this most beautiful temple, who would
> place this lamp in another or better position than
> that from which it can light up the whole thing at

the same time ? For, the sun is not inappropriately called by some people the lantern of the universe, its mind by others, and its ruler by still others. [Hermes] the Thrice Greatest labels it a visible god, and Sophocles' Electra, the all-seeing. Thus indeed, as though seated on a royal throne, the sun governs the family of planets revolving around it. Moreover, the Earth is not deprived of the moon's attendance. On the contrary, as Aristotle says in a work on animals, the moon has the closest kinship with the Earth. Meanwhile the Earth has intercourse with the sun, and is impregnated for its yearly parturition."

This quote from the man himself is quite revealing, isn't it?

COPERNICUS WAS CONSIDERED A FOOL
BY THE CHRISTIANS OF HIS DAY

The narrative that has been pushed hard in our public schools, our universities, textbooks, and even in the scientific community is that Copernicus was a genius who was admired for his discovery, and that his heliocentric theory was well accepted.[1] This goes along with the lie that "everyone knows the earth is a sphere that revolves around the sun, and everyone has known that from the beginning." This is a lie that has been pushed hard and continues to be pushed for the propaganda it is.

"Au contraire mon frère." Copernicus was considered a fool for blatantly disregarding the Bible's description of creation, and the battle lines were drawn between the Catholic Church fighting to promote heliocentrism and everyone else who did not accept heliocentrism, nor the idea that the Earth was a sphere.

Martin Luther wrote in Table Talk in 1539:

"There is talk of a new astrologer who wants to prove that the Earth moves and goes around instead of the sky, the sun, the moon, just as if somebody were moving in a carriage or ship might hold that he was sitting still and at rest while the Earth and the trees walked and moved. But that is how things are nowadays: when a man wishes to be clever he must . . . invent something special, and the way he does it must needs be the best! The fool wants to turn the whole art of astronomy upside-down. However, as the Holy Scripture tells us, so did Joshua bid the sun to stand still and not the Earth."

The opposition to Copernicus was phenomenal.

"All branches of the Protestant Church, Lutheran, Calvinist, and Anglican vied with each other in denouncing the Copernican doctrine as contrary to scripture and at a later time the Puritans showed the same tendency." Source: Andrew Dixon White, A History of the Warfare of Science with Theology, Volume 1, Page 126 (1897)

John Calvin had this to say:

"We will see some who are so deranged, not only in religion but who in all things reveal their monstrous nature, that they will say that the sun does not move, and that it is the Earth which shifts and turns. When we see such minds we must indeed confess that the devil posses them, and that God sets them before us as mirrors, in order to keep us in his fear." John Calvin, Sermon on 1st Corinthians 10:19-21, Calvini Opera Selecta, Corpus Reformatorum, Vol 19,077

With his heliocentric theory, Copernicus left any pretense of being involved in christian thought, and openly courted occultism with the full support of the Catholic Church.

THE PLANETS OF THE HELIOCENTRIC DESIGN

The word used for planets has the same Greek origin as the word used for deception ("planeo"). This is the same word used by Jesus to warn us of deception three times in Mathew 24. Another Greek meaning of the root word used for planet is "wanderer."

In the heliocentric system, the planets all wander in the "solar system"[2] and the Earth revolves around the sun at 66,600 miles per hour (notice the number 666 which is "the number of the beast"), and simultaneously the sun revolves around the center of the galaxy at 500,000 miles per hour, all the while the galaxy is traveling at 1.3 million miles per hour through the Universe.

God did not call the Earth a "planet" or any word whose derivative finds its root in "planeo". God called it the "Earth" and in Hebrew it looks like this in Strongs: "h0776. אֶרֶץ 'ereṣ; from an unused root probably meaning to be firm". In other words, when God speaks of the Earth, he describes it not as something that wanders, but as something that is firm or solid.

"Tremble before him, all the Earth; yes, the world is established; it shall never be moved." 1 Chronicles 16:30

Let's look closer at the planets. All of the planets were named after Greek and Roman gods and goddesses. God named Earth, but guess who named all the other planets. I'll give you one hint. It was not God. There's Jupiter,

Saturn, Mars, Venus, and Mercury. These were named thousands of years ago.

Mercury was named after the Roman god of travel. Venus was named after the Roman goddess of love and beauty. Mars was the Roman god of War. Jupiter was the king of the Roman gods, and Saturn was the Roman god of agriculture.

The other planets were named later when telescopes were available. Uranus was named after an ancient Greek king of the gods. Neptune was the Roman god of the sea. Pluto was the Roman god of the underworld.

Even though it was hundreds of years later, the same tradition of naming the planets after Greek and Roman gods was maintained for these later planets. Does this tell you anything about the plan that was implemented over such a long period?

How much more obvious could this Satanic scheme be right in our faces than it is? What an insult to God for the whole of creation to observe!

In the next chapters we'll look more closely at the planets and what they represent in this occult design.

---

1. There is the false narrative that seems to be in nearly every Copernicus biography that he was under attack from the Catholic Church, but that is not true, and it's part of the smoke screen they have tried to raise, primarily I think because they don't want anyone to know Copernicus' strong ties to the Catholic Church and that he was a religious heretic.
2. "Solar system" is in quotes in this book, because there is no "solar system." The Bible's full description of God's creation of the "heaven

and earth" does not include anything like a "solar system," nor does the Bible mention anything like "outer-space." Chapter 8 explains in detail God's precise description of the Earth, the open expanse above us, and the solid firmament over the Earth. The sun and the moon are "in the firmament" according to Genesis, and the stars and planets are also within or below the firmament. The sun is not the center of a "solar system," and the Earth and planets and asteroids and comets do not revolve around the sun. There is no "solar system."

THE ORIGIN OF THE WORD "PLANET"
MEDITATE ON THIS

The Greek origin of the word "planet" is another tell tale sign that Satan has been involved from the beginning of the heliocentric design.

"Planet" is related to the Greek word used by Jesus in Matthew 24:4 "planeo" which is translated as "deceit." Definitions from Thayer's Greek Lexicon, Strongs NT 4105: πλανάω:

a. to go astray, wander, roam about.
b. to lead away from the truth, to lead into error, to deceive.

Satan often reveals his evil schemes to the world blatantly while he mocks God in front of Heaven and Earth. By naming these celestial bodies "planets," with the meaning rooted in "deceit," he was broadcasting his plans to deceive the whole Earth centuries ago.

CHAPTER 6
MERCURY: PLANET OR GOD?

KEEPER OF THE BOUNDARIES BETWEEN THE UPPER AND LOWER WORLDS

Mercury is the smallest planet and the closest planet to the sun, but for our purposes these are the least interesting facts about Mercury. Mercury was named after an occultic god, a false god, a god that the ancients worshipped, and believe it or not, many still worship Mercury today.

In Greco-Egyptian mythology he was known as Hermes. The Romans knew him as Mercury, the son of Zeus and Maia. Zeus was the most powerful god of mythology, the god to whom all other gods answered. The ancient Babylonians called the planet, which was always visible to the naked eyes, Napu, after a god in their mythology.

Mercury was known as the god of financial gain (like the doctrine of demons known as the "prosperity doctrine"), commerce, eloquence, messages, communication, including divination through occultic rituals, and he was also known as the god of traveling, luck, trickery (sorcery), and thievery. He also was known as the guide of souls to the underworld, or the mediator between the realm of the dead and the kingdom of the living. His name means "keeper of boundaries," which is thought to come from his role as a bridge between the upper and lower worlds.

He was said to be born in a cave in Arcadia, a region in southern Greece, and is depicted as wearing winged sandals and a traveler's hat and carrying a magic wand. The wand was a caduceus, which is a winged staff with two snakes or serpents wound around it.

The caduceus staff was also used by some other gods, for example by the god Iris. It is a short staff entwined by two serpents, sometimes surmounted by wings. In Roman iconography, it was often depicted being carried in Mercury's left hand. It is hard not to see the obvious comparison of the serpents to "The Serpent" of the Garden of Eden.

It has been suggested that the oldest known imagery of the caduceus finds its origin in Mesopotamia with the Sumerian god Ningishzida. His symbol was the same staff with two snakes or serpents intertwined around it and dating back to 4000 BC to 3000 BC.

The myth is that the wand would wake the sleeping and send the awake to sleep. If applied to the dying, their death was gentle; if applied to the dead, they returned to life.

There is also a well known staff (the Rod of Asclepius)

with one snake or serpent which the American Medical Association has adopted as their symbol, which ought to raise a huge red flag for any thinking christian.

That staff known as the Rod of Asclepius has only one snake or serpent and is never depicted with wings. Even so, the caduceus is often used as a healthcare symbol. While some will vociferously differentiate the two staffs, their roots in the occult are so similar, I see no reason to distinguish them from a christian perspective.

Our healthcare system includes big pharma. The word "pharmacy" comes from the word "pharmakeia," which in Greek means "witchcraft or sorcery." Let's document that with this verse in Galatians:

Now the works of the flesh are manifest, which are these; Adultery, fornication, uncleanness, lasciviousness, Idolatry, **witchcraft**, hatred, variance, emulations, wrath, strife, seditions, heresies, Envyings, murders, drunkenness, revellings, and such like: of the which I tell you before, as I have also told you in time past, that they which do such things shall not inherit the kingdom of God. Galatians 5:19-21

The Greek word used for "witchcraft" in this verse is this word:

g5331. φαρμακεία pharmakeia; from 5332; medication ("pharmacy"), i.e. (by extension) magic (literally or figuratively): — sorcery, witchcraft.

It's a slow process, but we're putting the pieces of this massive evil jigsaw puzzle together. The more pieces we can fit, the more we understand.

The adoption by the medical community of such a satanic symbol is surprising, unless you keep digging. One survey found that 62% of professional healthcare associations used the rod of Asclepius as their symbol. The same survey found that 76% of commercial healthcare organizations used the Caduceus symbol.

In 1932, the following was written in The Scientific Monthly:

"As god of the high-road and the market-place
Hermes was perhaps above all else the patron of
commerce and the fat purse: as a corollary, he was
the special protector of the traveling salesman. As
spokesman for the gods, he not only brought peace
on Earth (occasionally even the peace of death), but
his silver-tongued eloquence could always make
the worse appear the better cause. From this latter
point of view, would not his symbol be suitable for /
certain Congressmen, all medical quacks, book
agents and purveyors of vacuum cleaners, rather
than for the straight-thinking, straight-speaking
therapeutist? As conductor of the dead to their
subterranean abode, his emblem would seem more

appropriate on a hearse than on a physician's car."
Source: Stuart L. Tyson, *The Caduceus*, in The Scientific Monthly in 1932

In honor of Asclepius, a particular type of non-venomous snake was often used in healing rituals, and these snakes were known as Aesculapian snakes. They crawled around on the floor in dormitories where the sick slept. These snakes were introduced at the founding of each new temple of Asclepius. From about 300 BC onwards, the cult of Asclepius grew in popularity and people came from all around to his healing temples. Source: Rod of Asclepius, Wikipedia, 2023

Archeological evidence from Pompeii suggests that Mercury was one of the most popular Roman gods. The gods typically had their own temples, or at least statutes of stone or precious metals that people could worship. Mercury's temple in Rome was built in 495 BC.

WHAT DOES THE BIBLE TELL US ABOUT MYTHOLOGY AND FALSE GODS?

The Bible has much to say on these subjects, and a deep Bible study on this subject is a worthy study. Keep in mind that the kind of belief systems behind Mercury, the naming of the other planets, and the creation of the heliocentric design involves many evil practices that the Bible warns us about, including:

sorcery, witchcraft, magic and black magic, black arts, wizardry, enchantment, necromancy, astrology, occultism, superstition, fortune-telling, horoscopy, voodooism, incantations, soothsaying, and divination

Here are some verses you already know, and I've included more in Appendix A.

Romans 1:25 Who changed the truth of God into a lie, and worshipped and served the creature more than the Creator, who is blessed for ever. Amen.

1 Timothy 4:1-2 Now the Spirit expressly says that in later times some will depart from the faith by devoting themselves to deceitful spirits and teachings of demons, 2 through the insincerity of liars whose consciences are seared.

Matthew 24:24 For false christs and false prophets will arise and perform great signs and wonders, so as to lead astray, if possible, even the elect.

THE NAMING OF MERCURY

The first known observation of Mercury is said to be by an Assyrian astronomer in the 14th century BC. Exactly when the Romans adopted the name Mercury is not known, but it was likely in the 1st millennium BC.

It should be obvious that no true believer would have participated in the naming of this planet after an occult god. Those who did were clearly also deeply invested in worshipping false gods.

In the earliest days of Mercury's assent as a false god in mythology, the heliocentric design had not yet come into existence. The majority of christians and the church fathers believed that the Earth was flat well beyond 1543 when Copernicus first published his theory in *On The Revolutions of The Heavenly Spheres*. Most rejected Copernicus' theory as nonsense and inconsistent with the Bible's version of creation.

As you will see as we continue to piece together this vast evil jigsaw puzzle, Mercury has a role to play today in the complicated evil script known as the heliocentric design, a script that was undoubtedly formed in the mind of Satan long ago.

One thing that should be abundantly clear: Mercury's name and it's history in mythology and all the worship it has received over the centuries is an affront to God the Creator who alone deserves our worship and devotion. God's wrath is coming to all those who worship Mercury.

Why on Earth would an astronomer in the 1st millennium, and even worse, all astronomers over many centuries, name all planets after anti-God occult gods? What does that tell you?

With all this in mind, how much do you as a believer want to be aligned to a heliocentric system that denies the God of Creation and insults him in the most offensive ways?

CHAPTER 7

VENUS: PLANET OR GOD?

GODDESS OF LOVE, DESIRE, SEX, AND FERTILITY

T he planet Venus is the second planet from the sun after Mercury, and is named after a Roman goddess.

In Roman mythology Venus is the goddess of love, beauty, desire, sex, fertility, prosperity, and victory. Venus was a key figure in many religious festivals, and was revered in Roman religion under numerous cult titles, including Aphrodite.

"The essence of Aphrodite's power was her ability to provoke desire. Sexual allure was long an intrinsic aspect of Aphrodite, and erotic pleasures were referred to as *ta Aphrodisia*, 'the business of Aphrodite.' The goddess's body was not fully revealed in Greek art, however, until about 350 B.C., when a sensational cult statue in her temple at

Knidos (in present-day Turkey), carved by the sculptor Praxiteles, represented her naked for the first time." Source: The Goddess of Love and Beauty, The J. Paul Getty Museum, Online Article as of Jan 2, 2023.

"Aphrodite held sway in many realms: sex, marriage, fertility, sailing, civic order, even war. The breadth and diversity of Aphrodite's powers meant that a single city might have multiple shrines, each dedicated to specific aspects of the goddess. The recurrent theme for her devotees—male and female, young and old—was her capacity to create harmony and union. This could be purely sexual, or could pertain to marriage or fertility." Source: Same

Venus became one of the most widely referenced deities of Greco-Roman mythology as the embodiment of love and sexuality. More than one temple was built in Rome devoted to praying to and worshipping Venus.

Venus' name and history in mythology and all the worship it has received over the centuries is an affront to God the Creator who alone deserves our worship and devotion.

THE POWER OF
HELIOCENTRISM
MEDITATE ON THIS

*Believing and endorsing the heliocentric system
    is no small matter to God.*

*Heliocentrism is Satan's counterfeit to God's
    creation story. All who glorify the heliocen-
    tric system honor Satan.*

*And all who glorify the heliocentric system
    dishonor and mock God the Creator.*

Fear God rather than man.

CHAPTER 8

THE EARTH IS NEITHER A PLANET NOR A SPHERE

EARTH WAS NAMED BY GOD WHEN HE CREATED IT.

W e started with the planet closest to the sun, Mercury, and we're moving through the planets to the furthest from the sun. The Earth is listed in the heliocentric model as the 3rd planet, but Earth is not a planet.

Secular astronomers have incorrectly defined Earth as a planet. The planets move about in circular patterns with the Earth at the center. Even the sun circles the Earth. But the Earth does not rotate, nor does it revolve according to the Bible.

The Bible has many verses that clearly state in black and white in both English and in the original Hebrew and Greek that:

- God placed the Earth and it hangs on nothing;
- The Earth has a foundation;

- The Earth never ever moves;
- The Earth sits on pillars;
- The Earth has four corners;
- The Earth has a cornerstone;
- The Earth has ends;
- The Earth is a circle;
- The firmament is a hardened substance;
- The firmament is above the Earth;
- The sun and moon are in the firmament;
- The Earth's livable space is contained within the firmament;
- God's throne sits on the firmament;
- God created the Earth, but the Earth is not a planet; and
- The sun rises and hurries back to its place, not the Earth.

Yes, the Bible says all these things, and much more. The Bible itself has the most amazing description of the creation of the Earth I have ever read.

As equally fascinating, the Bible does **not** even hint of a Copernican model that is heliocentric in which the Earth rotates around an axis at 1,037 mph at the equator, revolves around the sun at 66,600 mph, while simultaneously the sun (and the Earth and the planets) revolve around the center of the "solar system" at 500,000 mph, all while the "solar system" is carried by our galaxy at 1.3 million mph through the Universe.

"Solar system" is in quotes in this book, because there

is no "solar system." The Bible's full description of God's creation of the "heaven and earth" does not include anything like a "solar system," nor does the Bible mention anything like "outer-space." Chapter 8 explains in detail God's precise description of the Earth, the open expanse above us, and the solid firmament over the Earth. The sun and the moon are "in the firmament" according to Genesis, and the stars and planets are also within or below the firmament. The sun is not the center of a "solar system," and the Earth and planets and asteroids and comets do not revolve around the sun. There is no "solar system."

To believe the heliocentric model of the Universe, you would have to somehow be able to intellectually and spiritually take all these verses that God put in the Bible and either say they do not mean what they say, or you would have to perform some incredible intellectual gymnastics to come up with symbolic, allegorical, metaphorical, or poetic interpretations that deny their literal meaning. Such arguments do not survive basic hermeneutics.

Let me make a point: This is not about me trying to persuade you of anything—It is about you setting aside your pride and prejudices and looking directly to God's Word to understand what God himself said about how he created the Heavens and the Earth, and discerning God's truth from all the nonsense and lies we have been fed our whole lives in a world in which Satan is the god of this world.

First, we start in Genesis 1 with the raw creation story, and then we will examine the details. I'll use the KJV, although the ASV and for many verses certain other versions would be fine. I do not selectively use particular translations to prove a preconceived notion as some authors do, but I will avoid using a verse in a translation that has been translated with obvious error or bias. I imagine by now you have picked up on my passion for the Truth of God's Word, which means digging into the original languages in context, and using proper principles of interpretation. I encourage you to take each of these verses and do your own in depth study and compare Bible translations if you like.

In Genesis 1:1-5 God gives us this description of Earth's beginning:

In the beginning God created the heaven and the Earth. 2 And the Earth was without form, and void; and darkness was upon the face of the deep. And the Spirit of God moved upon the face of the waters. 3 And God said, Let there be light: and there was light. 4 And God saw the light, that it was good: and God divided the light from the darkness. 5 And God called the light Day, and the darkness he called Night. And the evening and the morning were the first day. Genesis 1:1-5

In Genesis 1:6-8 God creates the firmament:

And God said, Let there be a firmament in the midst of the waters, and let it divide the waters from the waters. 7 And God made the firmament, and divided the waters which were under the firmament from the waters which were above the firmament: and it was so. 8 And God called the firmament Heaven. And the evening and the morning were the second day. Genesis 1:6-8

In Genesis 1:9-13 God continues with the separation of the seas and the preparation of the land:

And God said, Let the waters under the heaven be gathered together unto one place, and let the dry land appear: and it was so. 10 And God called the dry land Earth; and the gathering together of the waters called he Seas: and God saw that it was good. 11 And God said, Let the Earth bring forth grass, the herb yielding seed, and the fruit tree yielding fruit after his kind, whose seed is in itself, upon the Earth: and it was so. 12 And the Earth brought forth grass, and herb yielding seed after his kind, and the tree yielding fruit, whose seed was in itself, after his kind: and God saw that it was good.

13 And the evening and the morning were the third day. Genesis 1:9-13

In Genesis 1:14-19 God created the sun and the moon and the stars:

And God said, Let there be lights in the firmament of the heaven to divide the day from the night; and let them be for signs, and for seasons, and for days, and years: 15 And let them be for lights in the firmament of the heaven to give light upon the Earth: and it was so. 16 And God made two great lights; the greater light to rule the day, and the lesser light to rule the night: he made the stars also. 17 And God set them in the firmament of the heaven to give light upon the Earth, 18 And to rule over the day and over the night, and to divide the light from the darkness: and God saw that it was good. 19 And the evening and the morning were the fourth day. Genesis 1:14-19

In Genesis 1:20-23 God created sea life and birds:

And God said, Let the waters bring forth abundantly the moving creature that hath life, and fowl that may fly above the Earth in the open firmament of heaven. 21 And God created great whales, and every living creature that moveth, which the waters brought forth abundantly, after their kind, and every winged fowl after his kind: and God saw that it was good. 22 And God blessed them, saying, Be fruitful, and multiply, and fill the waters in the seas, and let fowl multiply in the Earth. 23 And the evening and the morning were the fifth day. Genesis 1:20-23

In Genesis 1:24-25 God created animal life on land:

And God said, Let the Earth bring forth the living creature after his kind, cattle, and creeping thing, and beast of the Earth after his kind: and it was so. 25 And God made the beast of the Earth after his kind, and cattle after their kind, and every thing that creepeth upon the Earth after his kind: and God saw that it was good. Genesis 1:24-25

In Genesis 1:26-28 God created man and woman:

And God said, Let us make man in our image, after our likeness: and let them have dominion over the fish of the sea, and over the fowl of the air, and over the cattle, and over all the Earth, and over every creeping thing that creepeth upon the Earth. 27 So God created man in his own image, in the image of God created he him; male and female created he them. 28 And God blessed them, and God said unto them, Be fruitful, and multiply, and replenish the Earth, and subdue it: and have dominion over the fish of the sea, and over the fowl of the air, and over every living thing that moveth upon the Earth. Genesis 1:26-28

In Genesis 1:29-31 God provided food for man and animals:

And God said, Behold, I have given you every herb bearing seed, which is upon the face of all the Earth, and every tree, in the which is the fruit of a tree yielding seed; to you it shall be for meat. 30 And to every beast of the Earth, and to every fowl of the air, and to every thing that creepeth upon the Earth, wherein there is life, I have given every green herb for meat: and it was so. 31 And God saw every thing that he had made, and, behold, it was very good. And the evening and the morning were the sixth day. Genesis 1:29-31

68 CREATION VERSES

Having read the foundational verses that describe creation from Genesis 1, let's examine the following 68 verses, which give us more details of God's creation not exclusively revealed in Genesis 1.

These 68 verses describe the Earth as hanging where God placed it, having a foundation, never moving, sitting on pillars, having four corners, being on a cornerstone, having ends, and describes the firmament as a hardened substance above the Earth. To confirm these truths, let's make sure the Bible actually states these things unambiguously.

I used the ESV for these verses when I originally did this study, and I'll leave this translation intact for these 68 verses.

- Genesis 1:7 "Thus God made the firmament, and divided the waters which were under the firmament from the waters which were above the firmament; and it was so." In Job 37:18 it says "Can you, with Him, spread out the skies, Strong as a cast metal mirror? It is firm. In Proverbs 8:28 we are told "When He made firm the skies above, When the springs of the deep became fixed. In Genesis 1:6-8 it says "Then God said, 'Let there be an expanse in the midst of the waters, and let it separate the waters from the waters.' God made the expanse, and separated the waters that were below the expanse from the waters that were above the expanse; and it was so. God called the expanse 'heaven.'" In Psalm 148:4 it says "Praise Him, highest heavens, And the waters that are above the heavens!" The firmament is attached to the earth. In Amos 9:6 it says "The One who builds His upper chambers in the heavens And has founded His vaulted dome over the earth, He who calls for the waters of the sea And pours them out on the face of the earth, The LORD is His name." God placed the sun, moon and stars in the firmament. In Genesis 1:14-19 it says "Then God said, "Let there be lights in the expanse of the heavens to separate the day from the night, and they shall serve as signs and for seasons, and for days and years; and they shall serve as lights in the expanse of the heavens to give light on the earth"; and it was so. God made the two great lights, the greater light to govern the day, and the lesser light to govern the night; He made the stars also. God placed them in the expanse of the heavens to give light on the earth, and to govern the day and the night, and to separate the light from the darkness; and God saw that it was good. And there was evening and there was morning, a fourth day." In Psalm 19:1-6 it says "The heavens tell of the glory of God; And their expanse declares the work of His hands. Day to day pours forth speech, And night to night reveals knowledge. There is no speech, nor are there words; Their voice is not heard. Their line has gone out into all the earth, And their words to the end of the world. In them He has placed a tent for the sun, Which is like a groom coming out of his chamber; It rejoices like a strong person to run his course. Its rising is from one end of the heavens, And its circuit to the other end of them; And there is nothing hidden from its heat." His throne sits on the firmament. In Ezekiel 1:26 it says "And above the firmament that was over their heads was the likeness of a throne, as the appearance of a sapphire stone: and upon the likeness of the throne was the likeness as the appearance of a man above upon it." And in Isaiah 66:1 it says "Thus saith the LORD, The heaven is my throne, and the earth is my footstool: where is the house that ye build unto me? and where is the place of my rest?"

- Psalms 93:1 "The Lord reigns; he is robed in majesty; the Lord is robed; he has put on strength as his belt. Yes, the world is established; it shall never be moved." The fact that the earth has been "established" and that it "shall never be moved" is strong language indicating it cannot and will never move. That is exactly what the verse states. This verse cannot possibly be forced into an allegory.

- Psalms 96:10 "Say among the nations, 'The Lord reigns! Yes, the world is established; it shall never be moved; he will judge the peoples with equity.'"

- Psalms 104:5 "He set the earth on its foundations, so that it should never be moved." Why would God make sure the word "never" is in so many of these verses about earth's movement? I think God intended to use the word "never" so many times because he wanted to make the point that the way that he placed the earth is such that it shall "never be moved." That's hard to argue with, isn't it? I won't keep repeating this for all the verses, but this verse cannot possibly be forced into an allegory either.

- 1 Chronicles 16:29-30 "Worship the Lord in the splendor of holiness; tremble before him, all the earth; yes, the world is established; <u>it shall never be moved</u>." If God said it "shall" never be moved, then it must not revolve or rotate, unless God somehow forgot that it revolves and rotates. In law we learn the difference between "shall" and "will." "Shall" is mandatory, not optional like the word "will." Shall as used by God is a command, not a request. When God commands that the earth shall never move, it is a permanent command, not a request that could be adjusted or changed by astronomical forces beyond God's control.

- Job 26:7 "He stretches out the north over the void and <u>hangs the earth on nothing</u>." Why on earth would God say the earth "hangs on nothing" unless he was making a point he wanted us to understand? God put the earth in its place, and that's the end of it. There's no hint that the earth performs intergalactic gymnastics in these verses since God put the earth in its place and it never moves.

- Ecclesiastes 1:5 "The sun rises, and the sun goes down, and <u>hastens to the place where it rises</u>." The sun moves, and God wanted us to know this, but he mysteriously makes no mention of the earth moving, unless it doesn't move, in which case it's not mysterious that he doesn't mention that. Apparently God wanted to make a point by saying that the "sun hastens to the place where it rises." The word "hasten" connotes subservience, not dominance. If the sun hastens, it is not the greatest of stars, and if it hastens, perhaps it is subservient to the earth, rather than the earth being subservient to the sun. Why would God say the "sun hastens" to return if the earth as his greatest creation of all, rotates around the sun as its master?

- Genesis 1:14-19 "And God said, 'Let there be lights in the expanse of the Heavens to separate the day from the night. And let them be for signs and for seasons, and for days and years, 15 and let them be lights in the expanse of the Heavens to give light upon the earth.' And it was so. And God made the two great lights— the greater light to rule the day and the lesser light to rule the night—and the stars. And God <u>set them in the expanse of the Heavens</u> to give light on the earth, to rule over the day and over the night, and to separate the light from the darkness. And God saw that it was good. 19 And there was evening and there was morning, the fourth day." The expanse is the area below the firmament and above the surface of the earth.

- Proverbs 8:27 "When he established the heavens, I was there, When He <u>inscribed a circle on the face of the deep</u>." Circle is mentioned in describing the earth, but sphere is never used.
- Psalms 50:1 "The Mighty One, God the Lord, speaks and summons the earth from the rising of the sun to its setting." Again we have the sun moving, but no mention of the earth moving. There are no mistakes in the Bible.
- Deuteronomy 28:49 "The Lord will bring a nation against you from far away, from <u>the end of the earth</u>, swooping down like the eagle, a nation whose language you do not understand." Why would God mention the "end of the earth," which he does many times if the earth is a sphere? Do you think God is sloppy with the language? God is never sloppy with language.
- Deuteronomy 28:68 (ESV) "And the Lord will scatter you among all peoples, <u>from one end of the earth to the other</u>, and there you shall serve other gods of wood and stone, which neither you nor your fathers have known."

Commentary: There it is—from one end of the earth to the other end.

- Deuteronomy 33:17 "A firstborn bull—he has majesty, and his horns are the horns of a wild ox; with them he shall gore the peoples, all of them, to the <u>ends of the earth</u>; they are the ten thousands of Ephraim, and they are the thousands of Manasseh." How many times does God have to say "the ends of the earth" before we take him seriously? He says this in many verses, but . . . what . . . he didn't mean it?

- 1 Samuel 2:8 "He raises up the poor from the dust; he lifts the needy from the ash heap to make them sit with princes and inherit a seat of honor. For the <u>pillars of the earth</u> are the Lord's, and on them he has set the world."
Commentary: The earth was set on pillars, but tell me how we explain this away. God didn't mean pillars? Or it was just an expression? That doesn't make sense. What makes far more sense is that God meant what he said.

- 1 Samuel 2:10 "The adversaries of the Lord shall be broken to pieces; against them he will thunder in Heaven. The Lord will judge the <u>ends of the earth</u>; he will give strength to his king and exalt the horn of his anointed." For those who claim God's description of his own creation is allegory, it is getting virtually impossible to sustain that argument in the face of so many verses like this one.

- 2 Samuel 22:16 "Then the channels of the sea were seen; the <u>foundations of the world</u> were laid bare, at the rebuke of the Lord, at the blast of the breath of his nostrils." Picture what God describes with phrases like the ends of the earth and the foundations of the world. Are those consistent with descriptions of a sphere or a flat earth?

- Isaiah 5:26 "He will raise a signal for nations far away, and whistle for them from the <u>ends of the earth</u>; and behold, quickly, speedily they come!" Don't miss the phrase "ends of the earth."

- Isaiah 11:12 "He will raise a signal for the nations and will assemble the banished of Israel, and gather the dispersed of Judah from the <u>four corners of the earth</u>." God specifically used the phrase, "four corners of the earth," but you're going to tell me he didn't mean "four corners of the earth." What then did he mean? How can God possibly refer to four corners of a ball? Who in all of history has referred to the corners of a ball? No one, and God is the master of language.

- Isaiah 13:13 "Therefore I will make the Heavens tremble, and <u>the earth will be shaken out of its place</u>, at the wrath of the Lord of hosts in the day of his fierce anger." What? The earth has a place? According to God it does. The earth has a very specific place where he placed it.

- Isaiah 40:22 "It is he who sits above the <u>circle of the earth</u>, and its inhabitants are like grasshoppers; who stretches out the Heavens like a curtain, and spreads them like a tent to dwell in." "Circle" means circle, does it not. A circle is not a sphere. A plate is flat and it is circular. But it is not a sphere. A basketball is a sphere. In this verse, God sits above the circle. That's consistent with God's throne being on top of the firmament. It's also consistent with God looking down at a round or circular planet. This verse doesn't prove the earth is not a sphere, but again, what we read is that there are many verses that are consistent with a flat circular earth, and no verses that support the idea of a sphere. Do you not find that compelling?

- Isaiah 40:28 "Have you not known? Have you not heard? The Lord is the everlasting God, the Creator of the <u>ends of the earth</u>. He does not faint or grow weary; his understanding is unsearchable." Again we have God telling us the earth has "ends," and in case we think God forgot how he created the earth, the verse goes on to remind us that God's "understanding is unsearchable." He is all-wise and all-understanding, and we ought not to compromise his own words describing his creation. After all, God is a first hand witness to creation.

- Isaiah 41:5 "The coastlands have seen and are afraid; the ends of the earth tremble; they have drawn near and come." Are you beginning to recognize every occurrence of the phrase "ends of the earth"?
- Isaiah 40:22 "It is he who sits above the circle of the earth, and its inhabitants are like grasshoppers; who stretches out the heavens like a curtain, and spreads them like a tent to dwell in." Do not think I've pulled random verses out of thin air. When many verses refer to the earth as a circle rather than a sphere, that should tell you something.
- Isaiah 41:9 "You whom I took from the ends of the earth, and called from its farthest corners, saying to you, 'You are my servant, I have chosen you and not cast you off'". How do you explain away the "corners" of the earth? Allegory does not work here at all.
- Isaiah 42:10 "Sing to the Lord a new song, his praise from the end of the earth, you who go down to the sea, and all that fills it, the coastlands and their inhabitants." I haven't counted how many verses in the Bible say "end of the earth," but it's a large number.

- Isaiah 43:6 "I will say to the north, Give up, and to the south, Do not withhold; bring my sons from afar and my daughters from the end of the earth." Again and again. Repetition means something to God. It means he wants to emphasize a truth, and he does not want us to miss it.

- Isaiah 44:24 "Thus says the Lord, your Redeemer, who formed you from the womb: 'I am the Lord, who made all things, who alone stretched out the Heavens, who spread out the earth by myself.'" The words "stretched" and "spread" indicate pushing something out on a level or flat surface.

- Isaiah 45:22 "Turn to me and be saved, all the ends of the earth! For I am God, and there is no other."

- Isaiah 48:20 "Go out from Babylon, flee from Chaldea, declare this with a shout of joy, proclaim it, send it out to the end of the earth; say, 'The Lord has redeemed his servant Jacob!'"

- Isaiah 49:6 "He says: 'It is too light a thing that you should be my servant to raise up the tribes of Jacob and to bring back the preserved of Israel; I will make you as a light for the nations, that my salvation may reach to the end of the earth.'" Just a brief reminder here that a sphere has no "end of the earth." It's not possible.

Since when does God use words that don't fit the precise reality of what he is revealing? He never has in over 31,000 verses in the Bible.

- Isaiah 51:13 "And have forgotten the Lord, your Maker, who stretched out the Heavens and laid the foundations of the earth, and you fear continually all the day because of the wrath of the oppressor, when he sets himself to destroy? And where is the wrath of the oppressor?" Here God explains that he "stretched out the Heavens and laid the foundation of the earth." Does that sound like God the Creator is describing a spherical earth? Why in the world would the creator of the Heavens and the earth keep describing his own creation in a way that harkens back again and again to a flat perspective rather than a spherical one?

- Isaiah 52:10 "The Lord has bared his holy arm before the eyes of all the nations, and all the ends of the earth shall see the salvation of our God."

- Jeremiah 10:13 "When he utters his voice, there is a tumult of waters in the Heavens, and he makes the mist rise from the ends of the earth. He makes lightning for the rain, and he brings forth the wind from his storehouses."

- Jeremiah 16:19 "O Lord, my strength and my stronghold, my refuge in the day of trouble, to you shall the nations come from the ends of the earth and say: 'Our fathers have inherited nothing but lies, worthless things in which there is no profit.'"

- Jeremiah 25:31 "The clamor will resound to the ends of the earth, for the Lord has an indictment against the nations; he is entering into judgment with all flesh, and the wicked he will put to the sword, declares the Lord."

- Jeremiah 51:16 "When he utters his voice there is a tumult of waters in the Heavens, and he makes the mist rise from the ends of the earth. He makes lightning for the rain, and he brings forth the wind from his storehouses."

- 1 Samuel 2:8 "He raises up the poor from the dust; he lifts the needy from the ash heap to make them sit with princes and inherit a seat of honor. For the pillars of the earth are the Lord's, and on them he has set the world." I don't want you to miss the many verses, like this one, in which God clearly states without ambiguity that the earth has been "set" on "pillars." Brothers and sisters in Christ, that is NOT the image of a sphere, or even a hint of a sphere. On the contrary, it is an image that is NOT a sphere. Note that God repeatedly states the earth is on a foundation, set on pillars, has ends, and shall never move, and the only thing God doesn't say in the Bible is, "The earth is not a sphere." He has said everything but that, and for good reason. God never tries to save someone's soul by convincing them of facts. Instead, God invites you into a relationship by faith. Not proof, but faith. But he certainly did not hide the ball when he told us how he created the earth. People who choose to believe lies about creation do so intentionally and as an act of their own will, knowingly deciding to believe a lie against the truths of God's own description of his creation. Remember, ignorance of the law is no excuse, right?

- 1 Samuel 2:10 "The adversaries of the Lord shall be broken to pieces; against them he will thunder in Heaven. The Lord will judge the ends of the earth; he will give strength to his king and exalt the horn of his anointed."

- Job 9:6 "Who shakes the earth out of its place, and its pillars tremble."

- Job 11:7-9 "Can you find out the deep things of God? Can you find out the limit of the Almighty? 8 It is higher than Heaven—what can you do? Deeper than Sheol—what can you know? Its measure is longer than the earth and broader than the sea." The phrase "longer than the earth" is revealing. If the earth were a sphere, God could easily have said, "It's measure is greater than the earth's circumference," or he could have said, "It's measure is greater than the radius of the earth."

Why would God, who is so precise, and so meticulous, and so proud of his creation, describe it in so many ways that are consistent with flatness? Why would God misrepresent his creation so grossly if it were in fact a sphere? Would God, could God be so dishonest? May it never be!

- Job 26:10 "He has inscribed a circle on the face of the waters at the boundary between light and darkness." God knows that a circle is not a sphere or a ball.
- Proverbs 8:27 "When he established the heavens, I was there; when he drew a circle on the face of the deep." The imagery here is incredible. What image comes to mind? Drawing a circle on a flat surface, not a ball. God knew that is the image that would appear in our mind with this description. God never is deceptive, and he never misrepresents.
- Job 37:3 "Under the whole Heaven he lets it go, and his lightning to the corners of the earth." Since when does a sphere have corners? Tell me.
- Job 38:4-6 "Where were you when I laid the foundation of the earth? Tell me, if you have understanding. Who determined its measurements—surely you know! Or who stretched the line upon it? On what were its bases sunk, or who laid its cornerstone." There

is absolutely nothing in these verses that hints of a sphere.

- Job 38:13 "That it might take hold of <u>the skirts of the earth</u>, and the wicked be shaken out of it?" The mind does not construct a ball when reading this verse.
- Proverbs 17:24 "The discerning sets his face toward wisdom, but the eyes of a fool are on the <u>ends of the earth</u>."
- Proverbs 30:4 "Who has ascended to Heaven and come down? Who has gathered the wind in his fists? Who has wrapped up the waters in a garment? Who has established all the <u>ends of the earth</u>? What is his name, and what is his son's name? Surely you know!" Wow, can you hear in those words a God who demands to know from the arrogant how he created the earth? Do not think you can insult God on this subject of his carefully described creation? Do you want to mock him? Then declare the Bible's account of creation is all wrong and promote Satan's counterfeit version of creation.
- Psalms 18:15 "Then the channels of the sea were seen, and the <u>foundations of the world</u> were laid bare at your rebuke, O Lord, at the blast of the breath of your nostrils."
- Psalms 19:4-5 "Their voice goes out through all the earth, and their words to the <u>end of the world</u>. In them he has set a tent for the sun,

which comes out like a bridegroom leaving his chamber, and, like a strong man, runs its course with joy."

- Psalms 46:9 "He makes wars cease to the <u>end of the earth</u>; he breaks the bow and shatters the spear; he burns the chariots with fire."
- Psalms 48:10 "As your name, O God, so your praise reaches to the <u>ends of the earth</u>. Your right hand is filled with righteousness."
- Psalms 59:13 "Consume them in wrath; consume them till they are no more, that they may know that God rules over Jacob to the <u>ends of the earth</u>. Selah" This is strong language. It is more than a hint that God's wrath is coming for those who slander his creation.
- Psalms 61:2 "From the <u>end of the earth</u> I call to you when my heart is faint. Lead me to the rock that is higher than I."
- Psalms 65:5 "By awesome deeds you answer us with righteousness, O God of our salvation, the hope of all the <u>ends of the earth</u> and of the farthest seas."
- Psalms 67:7 "God shall bless us; let all the <u>ends of the earth</u> fear him!" Please don't forget to take all of these verses in context, and the phrases that refer to God's creation, phrases like "ends of the earth" are referencing creation in the context of the emphasis of the verse. In

this verse God references his creation and says "fear God."

- Psalms 72:8 "May he have dominion from sea to sea, and from the River to the <u>ends of the earth</u>!"
- Psalms 75:3 "When the earth totters, and all its inhabitants, it is I who keep steady <u>its pillars</u>. Selah" Here we have mention of God's creation of the earth, and his emphasis in this verse is God's power over all the earth and its inhabitants.
- Psalms 98:3 "He has remembered his steadfast love and faithfulness to the house of Israel. All the <u>ends of the earth</u> have seen the salvation of our God."
- Psalms 135:7 "He it is who makes the clouds rise at the <u>end of the earth</u>, who makes lightnings for the rain and brings forth the wind from his storehouses."
- Daniel 4:11 "The tree grew and became strong, and its top reached to Heaven, and it was visible to the <u>end of the whole earth</u>." This verse states that this tree was "visible to the end of the whole earth." That would not be possible unless the earth were flat or level.
- Micah 5:4 "And he shall stand and shepherd his flock in the strength of the Lord, in the majesty of the name of the Lord his God. And they shall

dwell secure, for now he shall be great to the <u>ends of the earth</u>."

- Zechariah 9:10 "I will cut off the chariot from Ephraim and the war horse from Jerusalem; and the battle bow shall be cut off, and he shall speak peace to the nations; his rule shall be from sea to sea, and from the River to the <u>ends of the earth</u>."

- Acts 13:47 "For so the Lord has commanded us, saying, 'I have made you a light for the Gentiles, that you may bring salvation to the <u>ends of the earth</u>.'"

- Revelation 7:1 "After this I saw four angels standing at the <u>four corners of the earth</u>, holding back the four winds of the earth, that no wind might blow on earth or sea or against any tree." Even the Heavenly angels in the last days during God's judgment will be talking about "the four corners of the earth." And if that wasn't enough, they will be "holding back the four winds of the earth."

- Revelation 20:7-8 "And when the thousand years are ended, Satan will be released from his prison 8 and will come out to deceive the nations that are at the <u>four corners of the earth</u>, Gog and Magog, to gather them for battle; their number is like the sand of the sea."

- Matthew 4:8 "Again, the devil took him to a very high mountain and <u>showed him all the</u>

kingdoms of the world and their glory." How would it even be possible that Satan "showed him all the kingdoms of the world" if the kingdoms of the earth curved around a sphere? This would only be possible if the earth were flat. To attempt to rebut that by suggesting Satan and Jesus could see through a spherical earth is pure speculation not supported by a single verse.

- Psalms 33:14 "From where he sits enthroned he looks out on all the inhabitants of the earth." Again, it would not be possible for God to see "all the inhabitants of the earth" if the earth were a sphere.

- Rev 1:7 "Behold, he is coming with the clouds, and every eye will see him, even those who pierced him, and all tribes of the earth will wail on account of him." Every eye will see him. That certainly suggests that we will all be looking up at Jesus when he returns. There's no suggestion of any kind that those on the other side of the earth will either be looking through the earth, nor is there any suggestion that we will somehow for the first time magically be able to see around a sphere to where Christ is visible. That's not in the verses. We would be making that up.

Once you're aware of how many times God talks about the ends of the Earth, the pillars, the foundation of the

Earth, how it hangs exactly where God placed it, that it shall not move, and so on, you cannot forget these verses, and you can't just blow them off as insignificant or just poetry or allegory. God has never been more forthright and as unambiguous as he is in these verses.

What is the Holy Spirit telling you? Do you feel comfortable ignoring all these Bible verses and going with Copernicus and NASA? More importantly, what do you think God thinks about your acceptance or rejection of his description of creation? Does your belief system on creation honor God, or does it mock God?

CHAPTER 9

MARS: PLANET OR GOD?
GOD OF WAR

Mars is the fourth planet from the sun. Since the Earth is not a planet according to the Bible, Mars is actually the 3rd planet from the sun. In ancient Roman religion and myth, Mars was the god of war and oddly enough, also a god of agriculture. He was pre-eminent among the Roman army's military gods.

Next I want to briefly point out some egregious history about this mythological god, Mars. The reason I want to do this is to show you how detailed the mythological reality was to the ancient cultures, and how much lore was developed in multiple cultures about all these false gods. This is important because this is only the tip of the iceberg. There are centuries of volumes upon volumes of detailed stories about each of the gods to the extent that much of what was written was believed to be historically true by unbelievers and those who lived in occultic practices.

The relevance of all this is that it also plays out for the incredibly detailed descriptions and fantasies of the heliocentric design. Those in the occult even today take these things dead serious, and they believe with all their souls that the heliocentric system is reality and that its "secret" meanings have great spiritual significance to them. Thank God their occultic secrets are now getting exposed by many who are writing and talking about these things.

Here's a brief bit of mythological history many believe is actually true.

In Rome's mythic genealogy and founding, Mars fathered Romulus and Remus through his rape of Rhea Silvia. His love affair with Venus symbolically reconciled two different traditions of Rome's founding; Venus was the divine mother of the hero Aeneas, celebrated as the Trojan refugee who "founded" Rome several generations before Romulus laid out the city walls . . .

In Classical Roman religion, Mars was invoked under several titles, and the first Roman emperor Augustus thoroughly integrated Mars into Imperial cult. The 4th-century Latin historian Ammianus Marcellinus treats Mars as one of several classical Roman deities who remained "cultic realities" up to his own time. Mars, and specifically Mars Ultor, was among the gods who received sacrifices from Julian, the only emperor to reject Christianity after the conversion of Constantine I. In 363 AD, in preparation for the Siege of Ctesiphon, Julian sacrificed ten "very fine" bulls to Mars Ultor. The tenth bull violated ritual protocol by attempting to break free, and when killed and examined, produced ill omens, among the many that were read at the end of Julian's reign. As represented by Ammianus, Julian swore never to make sacrifice to Mars again —a vow kept with his death a month later. Source: Mars (Mythology), Wikipedia

The Greek and Roman gods are blatantly immoral and evil. That is not hidden in their stories. Their behavior and their histories are intended to represent the dark side of the spirit world, and it is entirely justified to suggest that they symbolically represent Satan and his fallen angels and demons.

But notice that the history of these mythological gods records the stories as true and not just myths. That's because those in the occult believe in the false gods, worship the false gods, and believe the stories, if not literally, symbolically and more real than the True God and real biblical history.

IT'S NOT ABOUT THE PHYSICAL WORLD
MEDITATE ON THIS

*We seek to understand the meaning of the
planets and the sun from the heliocentric
narrative, and that is revealing, exposing,
and helps us to put what they are trying to
do in it's biblical perspective.*
But make no mistake:
*It's not about real estate—It's all about what
you believe.*

CHAPTER 10

JUPITER: PLANET OR GOD?

GOD OF THE SKY

Jupiter is the fifth planet from the Sun and the largest in the "solar system." Since the Earth is not a planet according to the Bible, Jupiter is actually the 4th planet from the sun. It is the third brightest natural object in the Earth's night sky after the Moon and Venus, and it has been observed since prehistoric times. It was named after Jupiter, the chief deity of ancient Roman religion.

In Roman mythology Jupiter is the god of the sky and thunder, and king of the gods in ancient Roman religion and mythology. Jupiter was the chief deity of the Roman state religion throughout the Republican and Imperial eras, until Christianity became the dominant religion of the Empire. The Romans considered Jupiter to be the equivalent of the Greek god Zeus.

In Roman mythology, he negotiates with Numa

Pompilius, the second king of Rome, to establish principles of Roman religion, like offerings and sacrifices.

Just like Americans swear an oath to God holding their right hand on the Bible, the Roman consuls swore their oath of office in Jupiter's name, and honored and worshipped him, and they prayed to Jupiter for guidance and success. Before the establishment of the Roman Emperor in 27 BC, the consuls held the highest political office in the Roman government. All of this is true, so one can conclude that these gods were false gods and this was occultic.

While the planet Jupiter in its physical reality can be differentiated from Jupiter the Roman god, it's important to recognize the powerful symbolism and meaning behind naming the planet after this god.

Sacrifices to Jupiter were made regularly, including the castrated bull ox, the lamb, and the wether (a castrated goat or castrated ram). The animals were required to be white.

These sacrifices to false gods is another example of how Satan counterfeits everything good that God does, including the Old Testament sacrifices that pointed to the future sacrifice of Jesus Christ on the cross as the true sacrificial Lamb.

The parallels and all the symbolism included with the naming of each planet and the central role of the sun, and of the entire heliocentric design must not escape you. Knowing the evil agenda behind the heliocentric design is vital to a christian who does not want to be in spiritual darkness about God's true creation story.

Each of the gods whom the planets are named after were worshipped and prayed to. We must recognize this for what it is—occult practices, sorcery, and the worship of false gods.

We cannot simply dismiss all of this as insignificant or of no importance to God. It is of vital importance to God. Notice in this verse how the context is God's own creation, and he is speaking for himself. His creation is important, and he will not share his glory with another.

This is what God the LORD says, Who created the heavens and stretched them out, Who spread out the Earth and its offspring, Who gives breath to the people on it And spirit to those who walk in it: "I am the LORD, I have called You in righteousness, I will also hold You by the hand and watch over You, And I will appoint You as a covenant to the people, As a light to the nations, To open blind eyes, To bring out prisoners from the dungeon And those who dwell in darkness from the prison. "I am the LORD, that is My name; I will not give My glory to another, Nor My praise to idols. Isaiah 42:5-8

Do you still think it's perfectly okay to believe in and promote the heliocentric system?

CHAPTER II

SATURN: PLANET OR GOD?

GOD OF TIME

S aturn is the 6th planet from the sun and the second largest in the "solar system". Since the Earth is not a planet according to the Bible, Saturn is actually the 5th planet from the sun.

In Roman mythology Saturn had two mistresses who represented different aspects of the god. The name of his wife, Ops, the Roman equivalent of Greek Rhea, means "wealth, abundance, resources." Saturn's other mistress was Lua ("destruction, dissolution, loosening"), a goddess who received the bloodied weapons of enemies destroyed in war.

Under Saturn's rule, humans enjoyed the spontaneous bounty of the Earth without labour in the "Golden Age" described by Hesiod and Ovid, and he became known as the god of time.

The potential cruelty of Saturn was enhanced by his

identification with Cronus, known for devouring his own children. Saturn was equated with the Carthaginian god Baal Hammon, to whom children were sacrificed.

You'll see in all of these gods a very dark and ugly side, an evil side that is the polar opposite of our Heavenly God. Who in their right mind would find delight in naming a planet after wicked and repulsive gods?

We have to ask ourselves, why on Earth would scientists who call themselves astronomers have such a passion to name every single planet after an evil god sending a message to the whole world that they reject the God of Creation and chose instead to mock him and his creation?

How sick would astronomers have to be to spend their lives designing an entire anti-God Universe complete with all the symbolism of God's polar opposite, Satan, and the imagery of fallen angels and demons as false gods? And how wicked would they have to be in their minds and spirits to glorify evil and mock a Holy God?

Don't think they didn't know the mythology and evil symbolism of the gods after which they named every single planet. Of course they knew.

As a prosecuting lawyer would present evidence to a judge, we will continue to amass the evidence in this case, and by the time we get all the evidence before you as the jury, I think you'll believe the heliocentric system is an evil design of the occult by clear and convincing evidence, and perhaps beyond a shadow of a doubt.

1 WANT TO KNOW THE TRUTH!

DO YOU?

"When I was a child, I used to speak like a child, think like a child, reason like a child. When I became a man, I did away with childish things. For now we see in a mirror dimly, but then face to face. Now I know in part, but then I will know fully just as I also have been fully known. But now abide faith, hope, love —these three; but the greatest of these is love." 1 Corinthians 13:11-13

CHAPTER 12

URANUS: PLANET OR GOD?

GOD OF THE SKY AND HEAVENS

U ranus is the seventh planet from the Sun. Since the Earth is not a planet according to the Bible, Uranis is actually the 6th planet from the sun. It is named after the Greek god Uranus (Caelus in Roman), who in Greek mythology is the father of Cronus (Saturn), a grandfather of Zeus (Jupiter) and great-grandfather of Ares (Mars).

As the mythology goes, Uranus mated with Gaia (the Greek Goddess and ancestral mother of all life on Earth), and She gave birth to the twelve Titans: Oceanus, Coeus, Crius, Hyperion, Iapetus, Theia, Rhea, Themis, Mnemosyne, Phoebe, Tethys and Cronus; the Cyclopes: Brontes, Steropes and Arges; and the Hecatoncheires ("Hundred-Handed Ones"): Cottus, Briareus, and Gyges.

Allow me to remind you how perverted these gods were and how bizarre the myths were:

According to the *Theogony*, when Cronus castrated Uranus, from Uranus' blood, which splattered onto the Earth, came the Erinyes (Furies), the Giants, and the Meliae. Also, according to the *Theogony*, Cronus threw the severed genitals into the sea, around which "a white foam spread" and "grew" into the goddess Aphrodite, although according to Homer, Aphrodite was the daughter of Zeus and Dione. Souce: Uranus (Mythology), Wikipedia

Deception is often built upon false history and myths with incredible detail, even with long family histories, and the characters are developed so that eventually followers identify with them until they become real people or real gods in their minds. You might be tempted to ask, "Who would believe all this mythology garbage?," and the answer would be, "millions throughout history who never knew God."

The intellectual argument of the occultists who love the evil histories of the mythological gods and the satanic symbolism inherent in the heliocentric design will argue that gods like Gaia were intended as personifications of the planets they represented, that they're not real, and it's all just fun and games.

Since when is it harmless fun and games to mock God? Is creating an entire counterfeit creation story that pretends there never was a God of creation just creative license? Is it just a minor affair that "scientists" (who are really pseudoscientists) insist that the Universe was created with a big bang, and that humans came from primordial soup?

We see how these gods have taken over Hollywood with the Disney movies starring Greek and Roman gods. Our children are being raised to admire these false gods with blockbuster movies, like "Thor," "Thor: The Dark," "Thor: Ragnarok," "Thor: Love and Thunder," "Clash of the Titans," "Wrath of the Titans," "Revenge of the Titans," "Gods of Egypt," "Along With The Gods," "Immortals," "Black Adam," "Hercules," "Troy," "Exodus: Gods and Kings," "Valhalla," "Wonder Woman," "Superman," "League of Gods," "Viking Destiny," "Hammer of the Gods," "Vikingdom," and many more.

These are not small matters if they are important to God, and I think we all know they are important to God. How can we understand these people who have created this parallel world in which God does not exist and they and their false gods reign? The Apostle Paul under the inspiration of the Holy Spirit stated the case better than me:

Romans 1:18-32 For the wrath of God is revealed from heaven against all ungodliness and unright- eousness of men, who by their unrighteousness suppress the truth.

For what can be known about God is plain to them, because God has shown it to them.

For his invisible attributes, namely, his eternal power and divine nature, have been clearly perceived, ever since the creation of the world, in the things that have been made. So they are without excuse.

For although they knew God, they did not honor him as God or give thanks to him, but they became futile in their thinking, and their foolish hearts were darkened.

Claiming to be wise, they became fools, and exchanged the glory of the immortal God for images resembling mortal man and birds and animals and creeping things. Therefore God gave them up in the lusts of their hearts to impurity, to the dishonoring of their bodies among themselves, because they exchanged the truth about God for a lie and worshiped and served the creature rather than the Creator, who is blessed forever! Amen.

For this reason God gave them up to dishonorable passions. For their women exchanged natural relations for those that are contrary to nature; and the men likewise gave up natural relations with women and were consumed with passion for one another, men committing shameless acts with men and receiving in themselves the due penalty for their error.

And since they did not see fit to acknowledge God, God gave them up to a debased mind to do what ought not to be done.

They were filled with all manner of unrighteousness, evil, covetousness, malice. They are full of envy, murder, strife, deceit, maliciousness. They are gossips, slanderers, haters of God, insolent, haughty, boastful, inventors of evil, disobedient to parents, foolish, faithless, heartless, ruthless. Though they know God's righteous decree that those who practice such things deserve to die, they not only do them but give approval to those who practice them.

CHAPTER 13

NEPTUNE: PLANET OR GOD?

GOD OF THE SEA

N eptune is the 8th planet from the sun, and it is the fourth largest and the farthest known planet in the "solar system." Since the Earth is not a planet according to the Bible, Neptune is actually the 7th planet from the sun. It is not visible to the unaided eye. Only five planets are visible with the naked eye and those are Saturn, Mercury, Venus, Mars and Jupiter.

Neptune is named after the Greek god Neptune. He is the counterpart of the Greek god Poseidon. In the Greek tradition, Neptune is a brother to Jupiter and Pluto, and *these two gods preside over the realms of heaven, the earthly world, including the underworld (hell), and the seas*. Neptune and Jupiter and Pluto replace God as the rulers of the realm of heaven and earth and the seas. Can you believe this? Do you see how unacceptable these myths are?

They are far worse than unacceptable! They are heresy, blasphemy, paganism, sacrilege, profane, immoral, apostasy, and stand opposed to everything good and Holy that we find in God.

What's astonishing is that we live in what we have believed is reality our whole lives, and yet this constructed false reality is reprehensible to God, denies God ever existed, and glorifies false gods and Satan.

Do you still want to believe in heliocentrism, especially when it is clearly not consistent with the Genesis story of creation? If you study the Bible and understand God's exact description of creation and how he created the Earth, our space, and the firmament, you would know you can no longer simply accept the Copernicus/NASA version any more, and the more you examine the real scientific evidence and recognize pseudoscience for what it is and the dominance of scientism (a false religion) in heliocentrism and in NASA's narrative, the more you begin to wake to the prospect that you have been hoodwinked just like millions of us have.

But when you examine how the so-called scientists and astronomers have named and designed the heliocentric version of creation, you see how it rejects the True God and promotes and glorifies false gods and a false narrative that puts man at the center of the Universe.

CHAPTER 14

THE SUN: STAR OR GOD?

THE SUN GOD IN HELIOCENTRISM

W e all know what the sun is, because we see it every day, unless it's cloudy. The misrepresentation of the sun in the heliocentric system is where scientism shines its brightest.

THE BIG LIE BY COPERNICUS & NASA

The Sun is a star at the center of the "solar system". The Sun's radius is about 432,000 miles, or 109 times that of Earth. Its mass is about 330,000 times that of Earth, comprising about 99.86% of the total mass of the "solar system". The sun is over 92 million miles from the Earth. The Earth and all the planets revolve around the Sun, and the Earth performs extraordinary gymnastics in outer-space.

The Earth rotates at 1,037 miles per hour at the equator on an axis that is 66 degrees from the ecliptic plane or 23.5 degrees from perpendicular, and the Earth "wobbles" on its axis. At the same time the Earth revolves around the sun at 66,600 miles per hour (note the number of the beast, 666) while the sun revolves around the center of the "solar system", while the entire galaxy travels through the Universe at 1.3 million miles per hour.

THE SUN'S ROLE IN THE HELIOCENTRIC DESIGN

The sun plays the part of the ancient sun god in this anti-God counterfeit of creation. It is placed at the center of the "solar system" with the Earth and all the planets playing subservient roles as they worship the sun god by revolving around the sun.

The Earth's insignificance is emphasized by how small it is compared to the sun, and how the Earth is at the Sun's mercy because of explosions on the Sun or solar flairs could cause great earthquakes or destroy the entire Earth, which could happen at any time randomly, reflecting the cruel and unpredictable nature of occult gods.

The Sun is pictured as great and mighty, and it's glorious description is intended to diminish the Earth as an insignificant random piece of junk in outer-space, the result of nothing more than a big bang 13.8 billion years ago.

Evolution is heralded as the meaningless power of the Universe that governs our lives amidst cruel and evil gods that serve their own pleasures and rule over us with little regard. Darwinian evolution fits hand-in-glove with a godless heliocentric system, completing the vision of humans as nothing but happenstance with no intrinsic value and no purposeful meaning in the Universe.

The primary Sun god is Helios, from whom they named the heliocentric system with the Sun as the center. In works authored by unbelievers who promote heliocentrism, you'll see them use the description of Helios as "the personification of the Sun," but what that really means to them is "the Sun god."

"Due to his position as the sun, [Helios] was believed to be an all-seeing witness, and thus was often invoked in oaths. He also played a significant part in ancient magic and spells. In art he is usually depicted as a beardless youth in a chiton holding a whip and driving his quadriga, accompanied by various other celestial gods such as Selene, Eos, or the stars. In ancient times he was worshipped in several places of ancient Greece, though his major cult centers were the island of Rhodes, of which he was patron god, Corinth and the greater Corinthia region. The Colossus of Rhodes, a gigantic statue of the god, adorned the port of Rhodes until it was destroyed in an earthquake, thereupon it was not built again." Source: Helios, Wikipedia

CASPIAN "CASPER" SARGINSON, J.D.

The role the Sun plays and the heliocentric design is all fiction, and what surprises many people is that there is no true science proving any of this.

Now let's go back to the Bible and find out how God described the Sun he created in the world he created.

THE BIBLE'S DESCRIPTION OF THE SUN

In Genesis 1 God created light on Earth dividing night and day on the first day, but he did not create the Sun and the Moon and the Stars until the 4th day.

> Genesis 1:14-19 And God said, Let there be lights in the firmament of the heaven to divide the day from the night; and let them be for signs, and for seasons, and for days, and years: And let them be for lights in the firmament of the heaven to give light upon the earth: and it was so. And God made two great lights; the greater light to rule the day, and the lesser light to rule the night: he made the stars also. And God set them in the firmament of the heaven to give light upon the earth, And to rule over the day and over the night, and to divide the light from the darkness: and God saw that it was good. And the evening and the morning were the fourth day.

- The Earth was created first, and the Earth was God's central creation, apart from man and woman later. The Sun was created later and clearly takes a subservient role to the Earth.

- God created the Sun to serve the Earth as a source of light, as he did with the Moon and the Stars. Again we are reminded the Sun is not greater than the Earth, but the Earth is greater than the Sun.

- The fact that the Sun is above the Earth and serves as a light also tells us the Sun is dwarfed by the size of the Earth, and that also indicates the Sun cannot possibly be 93 million miles from the Earth.

- We also learn there is something called the firmament, and God put the Sun "in the firmament." To make sure it is absolutely clear, God told us twice in these verses that the Sun is "in the firmament." The Sun is not under the firmament, nor above the firmament in some place never mentioned in the Bible, "outer-space." The Sun is "in the firmament."

- What is the firmament? The Bible tells us it is a hard crystalline like substance that God created to separate the waters below on the Earth from the waters above in the heavens. We are also told that God's throne sits right on top of the firmament.

- The Bible describes three heavens. The first is the space you and I live in, breathe, and see above us. The second heaven is the firmament itself. Yes, that's a little hard to understand why God would call the hard firmament "Heaven," but when you get to Heaven, you can ask him. The third Heaven is where God's throne is, above the firmament.

For a detailed biblical analysis of the firmament, read Appendix A: What is The Firmament?

So you can see that the Bible describes the Sun as God created it and placed it "in the firmament." One might get sloppy and say the Sun is within or under the firmament, but let's be careful about how God described his own creation to Moses in the book of Genesis. God did not say the Sun is within or under the firmament: He said it is "in the firmament."

This demolishes the nonsense that the Sun is 93 million miles from the earth and 109 times bigger than the Earth. And don't forget that secular anti-God scientists also say without any scientific evidence whatsoever that the Sun makes up 99.86% of the total mass of the "solar system". They don't just lie and make things up. They get incredibly bold and pretend to know that the Sun makes up not just an estimated 99% of the mass, but 99.86%! Unbelievable!

What else does the Bible tell us about the Sun's relationship to the Earth?

He stretches out the north over the void and hangs the earth on nothing. Job 26:7

We must take this verse serious. God hung the Earth on nothing. God did that! The Earth is not controlled by some "force" called gravity, and it isn't controlled by mysterious forces in the Universe. God hung the Earth, and it is still exactly where he put it. It was created by God and it exists by God's power.

But wait, it gets better. From 1 Chronicles 16:23-31:

Sing to the LORD, all the earth!
Tell of his salvation from day to day.
Declare his glory among the nations, his
marvelous works among all the peoples!
For great is the LORD, and greatly to be
*praised, and **he is to be feared above all***
gods.
*For **all the gods of the peoples are worthless***
idols, but the LORD made the heavens.
Splendor and majesty are before him; strength
and joy are in his place.
Ascribe to the LORD, O families of the peoples,
ascribe to the LORD glory and strength!
Ascribe to the LORD the glory due his
***name**; bring an offering and come*
before him!
Worship the LORD in the splendor of holiness;
tremble before him, all the earth;
*Yes, **the world is established; it shall never***
be moved.
Let the heavens be glad, and let the earth

CASPIAN "CASPER" SARGINSON, J.D.

rejoice, and let them say among the
*nations, "**The LORD reigns!**"*

Surely, these are some of the most beautiful words in all of the scriptures!

I'd like to highlight the obvious for your benefit. These verses start with a reminder that "all the Earth" is to sing to God, and we are told why. As the Creator who "made the heavens," God is to be greatly praised, to be feared "above all gods," (who we are reminded are "worthless idols"), and he is to be praised because he is Holy.

Then we are told that the Earth, the only identified "world" in the scriptures, "is established; it shall never be moved." This means that according to God, the Earth does not rotate, it doesn't wobble on an axis 66 degrees off the ecliptic plain, it doesn't revolve around the Sun at 66,600 miles per hour, and it doesn't travel with the Sun around the center of the "solar system" at over 500,000 mph, and it doesn't hurl through "outer-space" with our galaxy at 1.3 miles per hour.

The ecliptic plane is defined as the imaginary plane containing the Earth's orbit around the sun. In the course of a year, the sun's apparent path through the sky lies in this plane. The planetary bodies of our "solar system" all tend to lie near this plane, since they were formed from the sun's spinning, flattened, proto-planetary disk. Even NASA acknowledges that their ecliptic plane is "imaginary." Source: NASA Website

The Earth hangs exactly where God placed it, and it shall never move! Want more proof from the Bible?

The sun rises, and the sun goes down, and hastens to the place where it rises. Ecclesiastes 1:5

At last, we see the Sun is the celestial body that rotates around the Earth! Oh, how NASA and all the occultists and globers will hate me for sharing that.

Did you know Joshua asked God to stop the sun in its place while it was encircling the Earth so his army would have more sunlight to attack their enemies?

At that time Joshua spoke to the LORD in the day when the LORD gave the Amorites over to the sons of Israel, and he said in the sight of Israel,

> *"Sun, stand still at Gibeon, and moon, in the*
> *Valley of Aijalon."*
> *And the sun stood still, and the moon stopped,*
> *until the nation took vengeance on their*
> *enemies. Joshua 10:12-13 (ESV)*

The Sun is not the center of the "solar system". The Earth and the planets do not revolve around the Sun. The Earth is God's glorious creation, not the Sun.

For great is the LORD, and greatly to be
*praised, and **he is** to be feared above all*
gods.
For all the gods of the peoples are worthless
idols, but the LORD made the heavens.

WHO IS THE NO. 1 PROMOTER OF HELIOCENTRISM?
AND WHAT IS THEIR CONNECTION TO THE OCCULT?

The biggest promoter and advertiser of the heliocentric system is NASA hands down. Understanding the history of NASA's involvement in promoting the heliocentric system is the key to understanding their purpose.

CHAPTER 15

WHO IS NASA?

THE EARTH'S NUMBER ONE PROMOTER OF HELIOCENTRISM

N ASA has played a primary role in promoting the Earth as a sphere in the heliocentric model that denies God is the Creator. NASA has worked from their beginning to promote the big bang theory and the evolutionary theory of the Universe.

Understanding what is behind the heliocentric model of the Universe is vital for the Christian, because undergirding the heliocentric model with the Earth as a sphere is a powerful religion. The scientific community has long been behind this religion, although it is uniquely camouflaged as science (or pseudoscience). What it really should be called is "scientism," a religion focused primarily on using pseudoscience to prove that God does not exist, that this is a man-centered Universe, and that men have become gods on this Earth.

Consider this. Since NASA's official founding in 1958,

(and even earlier after WWII when the U.S. began the department that was to become NASA) it launched the largest public relations campaign in the history of the world. How did they do that?

NASA spent hundreds of billions of dollars over a period of decades to promote the Earth as a sphere and to promote their view of the Universe. Their view of the Universe is one without God. This is seen over and over again in their literature, on their websites, in the videos they produce, and in their documentaries. They have produced thousands of videos to affirm the heliocentric model. In all their work, NASA never misses the opportunity to remind us of the man-centered Universe.

This extensive 24/7 campaign put a globe of the Earth on the desk of almost every teacher in our public school system from Kindergarten through 12th grade. Every science book in the public schools has a very "scientific" approach full of godless opinions, atheist astronomers, and government agencies, all of which promote a purely secular view of the Universe.

God must not exist in NASA's $29 billion annual budget, because that would destroy over seven decades of money and effort to convince you and everyone else in America that God does not exist and you don't need God. Imagine what you could do if you had an advertising budget like that, $116 million dollars every work day of the week. Let there be no doubt—NASA is promoting a religion called scientism. NASA's view of creation is a Universe without God, and American citizens, including Christians, fund NASA's entire operation.

Why is it important that Christians have a biblical view of the Earth? Because the anti-biblical NASA view rejects all fundamental Bible doctrines, starting with the most important one—that God is the Creator of the Heavens and Earth.

Now you know why I say the flat Earth argument is so hot today, because we are right over the target so to speak. In other words, Satan doesn't want us convincing anyone that the Earth is flat, because that can open up unbelievers' eyes to the possibility that God does exist. This means there is no more important subject today than flat Earth.

NASA's Luciferian History

NASA's rocket program was started with a brain trust of rocket scientists who were Nazis under Hitler. After WWII the U.S. brought 200 Nazi rocket scientists to the U.S., gave them new identities and hired them as NASA scientists. Nazi Werner Von Braun was selected to lead the group as NASA's chief rocket scientist. All of this was done surreptitiously under a top secret project named "Project Paperclip." These Nazi scientists were given new identities, jobs at NASA with nice retirements, and never indicted for their war crimes.

If that was the end of the story, it would just be another disgusting example of a government program using tax dollars with no moral compass. But there is a deep dark secret behind all of this, and it is so evil, you are likely to be shocked when you know the full history.

Adolph Hitler was fascinated with the occult. He came into contact with people from the Thule Society, an occult organized after WWI, and when he rose to power over Germany, he brought in the best Luciferians from around the world who had experience communicating with demons. Why would Hitler do that?

Hitler had learned that there was "forbidden knowledge" that fallen angels brought to Earth in the antediluvian days, and he knew that much of that knowledge had been lost in the Great Flood. He learned from occultists that there were rituals they performed to break through into another dimension and communicate with demons or evil spirits. He also learned that these evil spirits knew things humans did not know, and that they had advanced knowledge of weaponry and secret rituals that could empower humans to build weapons unknown on the Earth.

These demonic powers were also believed capable of empowering people to overcome death and extend one's life span forever. These Nazi goals have not been lost to history, but simply taken over by billionaires of today who have been funding laboratories to discover a way to transfer human consciousness to a robotic body. You might also recognize this as man's attempt to achieve eternal life apart from God.

One of the keys to Germany's military success in rocket

science involved religious ceremonies, in particular satanic rituals. There have been stories of Nazis communicating with aliens or demons in underground tunnel systems. Of course, we don't have evidence to substantiate all the stories, but there is no doubt about Hitler's fascination and involvement with the occult, and there's no doubt he brought the occult into their weapons and rocket development. Believe it or not, these same goals are being pursued today at CERN, a scientific project that seeks to break through into another dimension in pursuit of the answers to the creation of life. The opening ceremony of CERN is still posted on Youtube and involved an extensive Luciferian ritual broadcast to the whole world.

The fact that the U.S. brought these Nazi scientists who were deeply entrenched in satanic ritualism from a German government with a leader who believed in the occult and the war against God should be of great concern to any Christian who has believed in NASA. The rhetorical question is, "Should you give NASA any credibility at all?," or "Should you believe anything NASA says and promotes considering their satanic background?"

If this was the end to the story, you might still feel there wasn't enough evidence to reject NASA or their heliocentric promotions, but there is much more.

ROCKET SCIENTIST JACK PARSONS

When the U.S. was first trying to get a rocket program off the ground, they leaned heavily on a man by the name of Jack Parsons. Here is Wikipedia's introduction to Jack Parsons:

John Whiteside Parsons (born **Marvel Whiteside Parsons**; October 2, 1914 to June 17, 1952) was an American rocket engineer, chemist, and Thelemite occultist. Associated with the California Institute of Technology (Caltech), Parsons was one of the principal founders of both the Jet Propulsion Laboratory (JPL) and the Aerojet Engineering Corporation. He invented the first rocket engine to use a castable, composite rocket propellant, and pioneered the advancement of both liquid-fuel and solid-fuel rockets.

Jack Parsons is credited for creating early rocket propulsion systems from his own laboratory and from the Jet Propulsion Laboratory. NASA relied heavily on the Jet Propulsion Laboratory for their rocket program. There's an interesting theory that Jet Propulsion Laboratories (JP Laboratories) was a play on Jack Parsons' name (JP Laboratories). Since Parsons was integral in the original rocket technologies at JPL, it seems more than just a mild coincidence.

Here's a quote from STSTW Media, which also includes information from many other credible historical sources:

Very few people across the world know that the space program of the United States should actually be credited to a Satanist, Jack Parsons, and not Werner Von Braun. The later was a German-American aerospace engineer and a pioneer of rocket technology in the US. Werner Von Braun was also a contemporary of Jack Parsons. Strangely though, most people of the later times never heard of Jack Parsons. . . . Werner Von Braun credited Jack with inventing the American space program. It was Jack who actually created the solid fuels that the US later used in the propulsion systems of Polaris nuclear missiles and in the Apollo space missions, according to a statement by Werner Von Braun.

While pioneering scientific developments that later put men on the moon, Jack was engaging in occult activities like the Ordo Templi Orientis (OTO). The notorious British occultist Aleister Crowley was leading OTO at that time.

Across Britain and the U.S., Crowley was said to be "the wickedest man in the world". It was at OTO that Jack and others took part in strange occult rituals like eating cakes prepared with menstrual blood. As his career progressed, Jack's interest in the occult grew manifold. In the early 1940s, Jack was appointed as the West Coast leader of the OTO. He pumped in money from his rocketry business into his occult activities. He even purchased a mansion in Pasadena to use as a den of hedonism. This gave him an opportunity to explore sexual adventures. [Source: ststworld.com]

Jack Parsons learned from the master of satanic rituals, Alister Crowley. Crowley combined all kinds of perverted and evil sexual acts during his satanic rituals in order to communicate with demons and gain power and secret knowledge. Crowley was Parsons' spiritual mentor, and these methods were taught to Parsons who practiced them in his Pasadena mansion.

Jack Parsons was joined by the famous L. Ron Hubbard, who later became the founder of the Church of Scientology. They became best friends, and Hubbard joined Parsons in his satanic rituals on the Pasadena property.

It is believed that Crowley, based on his own writings, did actually learn to break through spiritual dimensions in which he would communicate with demons who shared secret knowledge with him and from whom he allegedly acquired spiritual powers. Parsons and Hubbard learned from Crowley how to perform the rituals necessary to communicate with demons or evil spirits. Allegedly the two men accomplished this on the Pasadena property, but they could not close the portal they had opened, and there is much speculation about what came through that portal. In any event, they both promptly retreated from further efforts to reach the satanic side, and shortly thereafter Parsons died at 37 years old in his own laboratory, supposedly from an explosion.

Much more could be written about these evil men and their satanic practices, but let's connect the dots to NASA.

Crowley, Parsons, and Hubbard were evil men who practiced satanic rituals to communicate with and learn from demonic spirits. They claim to have been successful in those regards, and Parsons did introduce the U.S. to new inventions that developed our early rocket technologies. Parsons was a key scientist with the Jet Propulsion Laboratory, still an important force in American rocket and space technology.

Then we have Werner Von Braun and 200 other Nazi rocket scientists who served Hitler faithfully to the very end of WWII, who were hired secretly by the U.S. Government and were employed in what later became NASA.

As a mature Christian, are you going to tell me now that you believe anything and everything NASA tells you? Whom do you believe, an organization that clearly was founded with satanic principles and evil men, or the Bible which explains clearly how God created the Earth?

NASA has not changed its original agenda. Even today NASA continuously promotes the man-centric anti-God view of creation and the Universe, and they milk the heliocentric model every chance they get.

CHAPTER 16

PUTTING TOGETHER THE HELIOCENTRIC SCHEME

IT'S ALL ABOUT WHAT YOU BELIEVE

I f everyone knew that God created the Heavens and the earth, and if everyone knew precisely how God created the Heavens and the earth, and if everyone could clearly see God's handiwork in the world, who wouldn't believe in God?

For you theologians out there who might say, "Well, don't forget about predestination. Even if creation by God was obvious and Satan never tried to cover it up or create a false narrative, faith is still a gift from God and God chooses those who will have eyes to see and ears to hear. Those not predestined and not chosen by God will be blind and will never acknowledge God or the death of Christ for our salvation." True, but I want to share logical thinking that is Biblical and makes a bigger point—that Satan has a purpose and reason to cover up the real creation story.

Perhaps a better way to express the thought is this. If

we weren't deceived so effectively our whole lives, we wouldn't be easily fooled into looking everywhere for life except to God the Creator.

If you remove God from creation, there is no God, and the rest of the Bible is irrelevant.

The Bible actually reveals a lot about Satan. It tells us about Satan's fall from Heaven, his temptation of Eve in the Garden of Eden, his method of drawing Adam and Eve away from God, his own pride and how he uses that same fleshly tendency in humans to cause them to turn away from total dependence upon God to Satan and to their own flesh.

From the beginning Satan made it clear that his emphasis, his whole focus and his entire strategy was to get humans to do what he had already done—turn away from God to his own knowledge and his own reality. Satan told Eve, "For God knows that in the day you eat from it your eyes will be opened, and you will be like God, knowing good and evil." [Genesis 3:5]

When used as a proper name, the Hebrew word, Satan, means "the adversary" (Job 1:6-12 and 2:1-7). In the New Testament it is used interchangeably with "Diabolos," or the devil, more than thirty times. Easton's Bible Dictionary clarifies Satan's character:

He is also called "the dragon," "the old serpent" (Revelation 12:9; 20:2); "the prince of this world" (John 12:31; 14:30); "the prince of the power of the air" (Ephesians 2:2); "the god of this world" (2 Corinthians 4:4); "the spirit that now worketh in the children of disobedience" (Ephesians 2:2). The distinct personality of Satan and his activity among men are thus obviously recognized. He tempted our Lord in the wilderness (Matthew 4:1-11). He is "Beelzebub, the prince of the devils" (12:24). He is "the constant enemy of God, of Christ, of the divine kingdom, of the followers of Christ, and of all truth; full of falsehood and all malice, and exciting and seducing to evil in every possible way." His power is very great in the world. He is a "roaring lion, seeking whom he may devour" (1 Peter 5:8). Men are said to be "taken captive by him" (2 Timothy 2:26). Christians are warned against his "devices" (2 Corinthians 2:11), and called on to "resist" him (James 4:7). Christ redeems his people from "him that had the power of death, that is, the devil" (Hebrews 2:14). Satan has the "power of death," not as lord, but simply as executioner.

In Genesis 3:1 we are told that "the serpent was more crafty than any beast of the field which the Lord God had made." This means that Satan is the craftiest evil being to ever exist. This is what you and I are up against. Satan is so much smarter and craftier than you and me, we cannot in our wildest imaginations keep up with the wiles of the devil. Don't think for a minute you can take on the devil and win. He's been at this for a hundred thousand of your lifetimes.

What was Satan trying to do from day one in the Garden of Eden? He fully intended to draw the first man and woman God created away from the Creator, and to distort their understanding of God and of his creation. Satan did this with lies about knowledge!

Satan knew from the beginning how Adam and Eve were created and what motivated them, and he knew their weaknesses. This is evident in Genesis 3 verse 6:

When the woman saw that the tree was good for food, and that it was a delight to the eyes, and that the tree was desirable to make one wise, she took from its fruit and ate; and she gave also to her husband with her, and he ate. Genesis 3:6

Don't miss the big revelation in these early Genesis verses about human character and our greatest weaknesses. It's right there in the third chapter of the Bible in three abundantly clear points.

First, Eve saw that the tree was good for food, meaning it brought the physical body great fulfillment. Second, she saw that the tree was a delight to the eyes, meaning the eyes fed the lusts of the heart. Third, Eve saw that the tree was desirable to make one wise, meaning it met another human need—the need to fill that God-shaped vacuum, that hunger that has always driven men and women to chase after that "something" that will finally make them happy. From the very beginning through all of time men and women have chased lusts and money and power, rather than seek peace in the only place it can be found—in a relationship with God.

But notice that Satan was pulling Eve away from God in all three of the main areas that motivated her as a human being, and she quickly ran with the temptation. These are the same three areas that still motivate human beings to turn away from God today. Later we learn that Satan "deceived" Eve in this way. Don't forget that word "deceived" or "deception."

Do you think Satan might have been working since the fall in the Garden of Eden to continue to persuade you and every human God created that Satan's reality is better than God's? Do you think Satan has been successful in getting humans to believe that human knowledge is the true knowledge, and that they can educate and teach themselves the way things are, and that the Bible is not necessary because there is no God?

That is Satan's most fundamental goal—to get you
and every human being on earth to believe there is

no God. There it is, out in the open now. That is one of Satan's most important goals.

Satan is the craftiest of all created beings, and he knows that if you believe in him, you will also believe there is a real God, so he has been diligently working for thousands of years to make sure no one thinks he is real either.

Enter the secular anti-god scientists and philosophers. Enter Copernicus with the first complete secular model of the Heavens and the earth that totally denied there is a God of creation. Enter Werner Von Braun (Nazi Scientist) who supervised NASA's early rocket science division with his fellow Nazi scientists, and who put meat on the bones of the Copernicus heliocentric model of creation where there is not only no God, but where happenstance is the first rule of creation with a big bang that is itself unexplainable by their own laws of physics.

President Truman agreed to hire Hitler's scientists (200 of them) and bring them to the U.S., give them new identifies and jobs running a new organization called NASA. This ought to make NASA suspect from the very beginning of its inception. Remember, Hitler and his scientists were heavily involved in the occult, and it was Satan, not God, who played the primary role in determining their theories of creation, science, and warfare.

Notice they didn't just leave God out of creation (where all the planets are named after Greek and Roman gods and goddesses), they also left out any mention of Satan.

By the way, Earth is not a planet. The Bible states that the earth does not move, that God hung the earth on nothing, and that the sun hurries back and forth in its movement, but the earth does not move. The meaning of "Planet" goes to the root meaning for "wanderer."

Both God and Satan are conspicuously missing from any account of creation promoted by NASA, Copernicus, the education system, the main street media, and the anti-god scientific community. How convenient!

I hope you have not missed another obvious counterfeit Satan implemented in the heliocentric design. Notice that the attributes, the character, and the personification of all the Greek and Roman gods and goddesses are counterfeits of the One and Only True God.

Let me briefly explain with these bullet points:

- Mercury is the keeper of the boundaries between the upper and lower worlds. Actually God is.
- Venus is the goddess of love, desire, sex and fertility. Actually God is creator of all these.
- Mars is the god of war, but God is the real God of War whose wrath was seen when he flooded the entire earth, and whose wrath will come again in judgment.
- Jupiter is the god of the sky, but who really is the God of the sky? God's throne sits on the firmament above the sky.

- Saturn is the god of time, but no one is the master of time except the One True God "who is and who was and who is to come, the Almighty." Revelation 1:8
- Uranus is the god of the sky and heavens. The truth is there is only One God, and "In the beginning God created the heavens and the earth." Genesis 1:1
- Neptune is the god of the sea, but only the True "God created the great sea creatures and every living creature that moves, with which the waters swarmed, according to their kind, and every winged bird according to its kind; and God saw that it was good." Genesis 1:21
- Helios is the sun god, but it was on the 4th day of creation when the God of Creation created "the greater light to govern the day." Genesis 1:16

Throughout the details and the entire design of the heliocentric system, Satan looked to God for inspiration and for creative ideas that would resonate with God's human race. There is only One True God of Creation, and Satan is not him. Satan is nothing but an angry counterfeiter masquerading as a great sorcerer whose sycophants bow down and worship him . . . for now. But soon, "At the name of Jesus every knee will bow, of those who are in heaven and on earth and under the earth, and every tongue will confess that Jesus Christ is Lord, to the glory of God the Father." Philippians 2:10-11

Amen to that! Evil will not dominate this world forever. The War of the Ages does have an end, and the earthly reign of Satan and all the fallen angels will come to a violent end, and on the day of judgment, they will be cast into the Lake of Fire for all of eternity! Hallelujah!

HELIOCENTRISM AND EVOLUTION ARE EVIL PARTNERS

What fertile soil Darwin had for his wild theories! Of course, to believe Darwin's theories you have to believe there is no God, no Satan, and that the whole Universe is nothing more than a series of extraordinary coincidences that are mathematically impossible even after billions of years.

I give you NASA's model of the earth, the sun and the moon, and the stars and the planets. This complex model, undoubtedly the creation of evil geniuses, fits Satan's comprehensive strategy perfectly.

The last thing Satan wants you to think is that God created the Heavens and the earth, and that he did it precisely as described in the Bible. Americans have taken Satan's bait hook, line, and sinker. Not only that, they get angry if you suggest the earth is not a globe revolving around the sun. So thoroughly brainwashed are the majority of Americans, they vociferously argue that NASA's pseudoscience rules over the Word of God. Of course, they would deny that, but one only needs to examine their beliefs to draw that inevitable conclusion.

What say you? Will you believe the literal description by God himself in Genesis, or do you prefer to believe Satan's counterfeit version of creation?

CHAPTER 17

GOD WILL NOT SHARE HIS GLORY WITH ANOTHER

I f you live under the belief that God created a heliocentric system and that the Earth is a sphere, you need to know that the Bible describes that first as idol worship and secondly as giving God's glory to another (Satan). Both are extremely serious offenses against God alone, and I'll prove that here with God's own words.

God wants every single believer to know that he will not share his glory with another, and he will most certainly not share the glory of his creation of "heaven and Earth," nor his self-revelation of his power and authority that is his alone manifested in creation.

I am the LORD, that is My name; I will not give My glory to another, Nor My praise to idols. Isaiah 42:8

For My own sake, for My own sake, I will act; For how can My name be profaned? And I will not give My glory to another. Isaiah 48:11

In the very beginning of the Bible what story did God choose to tell us first? Genesis 1:1 starts with, "In the beginning God created the heaven and the earth."

God wanted us to know that he was the Creator of the heaven and the Earth and that he is also our Creator. In fact, he tells us he was the Creator of all that was created.

In fact, the creation story is God's revelation of himself to us, of his eternal nature, of his power, of his authority, of his creativity, of his beauty, and of his glory.

The heavens declare the glory of God; the skies proclaim the work of his hands. Psalm 19:1

Through him all things were made; without him nothing was made that has been made. John 1:3

For the Lord is the great God, the great King above all gods. In his hand are the depths of the earth, and the mountain peaks belong to him. The sea is his, for he made it, and his hands formed the dry land. Psalm 95:3-5

For since the creation of the world God's invisible qualities—his eternal power and divine nature—have been clearly seen, being understood from what has been made, so that people are without excuse. Romans 1:20

How many are your works, Lord! In wisdom you made them all; the earth is full of your creatures. There is the sea, vast and spacious, teeming with creatures beyond number—living things both large and small. Psalm 104:24-25

How can we know God intended to connect his creation of heaven and Earth with the idea that will not share his glory with another?

Remember this verse in Isaiah:

For My own sake, for My own sake, I will act; For how can My name be profaned? And I will not give My glory to another. Isaiah 48:11

The very next verse makes the connection:

Listen to Me, Jacob, Israel whom I called; I am He, I am the first, I am also the last. Assuredly My hand founded the earth, And My right hand spread out the heavens; When I call to them, they stand together. Isaiah 48:12-13

When God says he won't share his glory with another, he finishes his thought by emphasizing that his hand founded the earth and his right hand spread out the heavens.

Notice the context when we examine this verse from Isaiah:

I am the LORD, that is My name; I will not give My glory to another, Nor My praise to idols. Isaiah 42:8

God will not stand for us to praise idols, and a sphere earth is not only a graven image, a globe that represents Satan's counterfeit creation, it also represents the heliocentric occult creation of Satan with all of its false gods and goddesses, and the false Universe that millions of believers falsely credit to God.

Can you imagine how this offends a Holy God who created the heaven and Earth, and described exactly how he created it in Genesis, not only in Genesis but with many other verses throughout the Bible? Yet we disregard his precise description, which is geocentric in plain language, and which is geocentric under fundamental rules of interpretation via proper hermeneutics and exegesis. Nowhere in the Bible is the earth described as a globe or in a heliocentric Universe. Absolutely nowhere. Not one verse.

Sing to the LORD a new song, Sing His praise from the end of the earth! You who go down to the sea, and all that is in it; You islands, and those who live on them. Isaiah 42:10

Not only will God not give his glory to another, and not only will he specifically not give his glory in creation to another, he reminds us in Isaiah 42:10 that we are to sing his praises . . . where? "From the end of the earth! You who go down to the sea, and all that is in it; You islands, and those who live on them."

In other words, we are to praise him and glorify him for his creation and as we see and live in his beautiful creation.

God has not allowed us to miss who he is in creation. He made it clear:

For since the creation of the world God's invisible qualities—his eternal power and divine nature—have been clearly seen, being understood from what has been made, so that people are without excuse. Romans 1:20

God will **not** share his glory with another! And God does **not** allow us to worship idols or graven images. If you own a small globe of the earth or any representation of a globe earth, I strongly recommend you destroy it immediately.

Do not give Satan glory by honoring his counterfeit creation known as the heliocentric Universe and the globe Earth.

I recommend you take this serious, because God takes this deadly serious, and the context of Isaiah from chapter 24 to the end of Isaiah is God's coming wrath and judgment against sin and an entire world that has turned against him.

But there is one very significant point God wanted us to understand, and because so many believers have been deceived by heliocentrism, they have completely missed the meaning and power of this next verse.

Then the moon will be humiliated and the sun ashamed, For Yahweh of hosts will reign on Mount Zion and in Jerusalem, And His glory will be before His elders. Isaiah 24:23

Because so many theologians and pastors have been deceived to believe in heliocentrism and a globe earth, just like the rest of us, they have either ignored this verse entirely because they didn't know what to do with it, or as in the case of the great John Calvin, grossly misinterpreted it with a speculation not supported in the context.

The context of Isaiah 24:23 is the beginning of God's judgment upon the earth, which is likely during the seven year tribulation. John Calvin understood that, but he went on to suggest that the reason the moon will be humiliated and the sun ashamed is because the glory of the Lord who returns to rule on earth in his millennial kingdom is so gloriously bright, the lights of the moon and sun will be diminished.

But that is nonsense, and it is horrible hermeneutics. I'll briefly explain why.

There's no doubt the glory of the Lord will be bright, so bright no sun will be needed to fill the earth with light. But that's not what this verse says. This verse doesn't state the light of the moon will be "overcome" or the light of the sun will be "diminished" by the glory of the Lord.

The word "humiliated" and the word "ashamed" clearly have meanings completely different than overcome or diminished. You are humiliated or ashamed when you have done something very wrong, and now you are exposed by the foolishness of your wrongful behavior for all to see.

"Ashamed" is defined in a Hebrew Lexicon as follows:

1) to put to shame, be ashamed, be disconcerted, be disappointed

This is consistent with our modern definition of "ashamed" from the Miriam-Webster Dictionary, "feeling shame, guilt, or disgrace."

Now, no one would claim the moon or the sun have feelings like a person. They are inanimate objects, not humans created after the image of God. So the use of these words, "humiliated" and "ashamed" are clearly intended metaphorically. We could also say that everything created by God is subject to God, upheld by God's power, and creation recognizes it's creator, not with a mind that thinks, but with the very elements of it's existence.

Since the sun and the moon were used in Satan's false heliocentric Universe as false idols, and in particular the sun as a false god, and since the sun played a particularly significant role as Helios, the sun god worshipped by the other planets (all named after Greek gods and goddesses)

with the sun at the center and all others revolving around the sun, serving and worshipping the sun in Satan's heliocentric occultic model, the moon and sun will be exposed for the deceptive and evil roles that they played.

Their roles will be revealed for all to see when Satan and all his evil deceptions are exposed by the King when he returns in judgment to destroy the Earth that has been under the rule of Satan, the god of this world. Jesus will recreate the earth to represent the truth about him and creation and all will glorify him again.

As always, we take the meaning of a verse directly from the verse in its context, and immediately after describing the humiliation of the moon and the sun as ashamed (Isaiah 24:23), we are told that Jesus will reign on Mount Zion in Jerusalem, and . . . His glory will be before His elders.

The moon and the sun were not described as humiliated and ashamed metaphorically because they were outshined by Jesus glory, but because of the shameful role they played in Satan's deception of generations of God's people, playing a major role in turning people away from God as the Creator, persuading people there is no God but only a Big Bang, and with heliocentrism's ally, Darwinian Evolution, humans are no more than primordial slop that became life without meaning and without purpose.

All of God's creation is subject to him, because he created it from nothing. Throughout the scriptures we see that God's creation bows down to him and praises him as the Creator. Here it is in Psalm 148:

Praise the LORD!
Praise the LORD from the heavens;
Praise Him in the heights!
Praise Him, all His angels;
Praise Him, all His heavenly armies!
Praise Him, sun and moon;
Praise Him, all stars of light!
Praise Him, highest heavens,
And the waters that are above the heavens!
They are to praise the name of the LORD,
For He commanded and they were created.
He has also established them forever and ever;
He has made a decree, and it will not pass
*   away.*
Praise the LORD from the earth,
Sea monsters, and all the ocean depths;
Fire and hail, snow and clouds;
Stormy wind, fulfilling His word;
Mountains and all hills;
Fruit trees and all cedars;
Animals and all cattle;
Crawling things and winged fowl;
Kings of the earth and all peoples;
Rulers and all judges of the earth;
Both young men and virgins;
Old men and children.
They are to praise the name of the LORD,
For His name alone is exalted;
His majesty is above earth and heaven.

And He has lifted up a horn for His people,
Praise for all His godly ones,
For the sons of Israel, a people near to Him.
Praise the LORD! Psalms 148 (NASB 2020)

God created the heaven and the Earth. He will not share his glory with another, least of all Satan. He will not have you worshipping false images, nor will he stand for you adoring a counterfeit of his glorious creation, called heliocentrism with a globe Earth that is not at all like the Earth he created for us to inhabit.

Make no mistake, it matters to God whether you believe in geocentrism or heliocentrism. In fact, it is of grave importance to God. Therefore, it ought to be of grave importance to you, too.

CHAPTER 18

SATAN'S MASSIVE DECEPTION IS ABOUT TO COLLAPSE

IT'S TIME FOR THE 2ND REFORMATION

Satan has invested everything he has in the greatest deception in human history, the heliocentric system. If his deception is successfully exposed to millions upon millions of people whose eyes are opened, and who turn away from this massive deception, Satan's world of sorcery will collapse. The curtain will be pulled open to expose the wizard.

People everywhere will realize they have been lied to about almost everything where Satan is the god of this world. The biggest deception in history will lose its power over people, and Satan will lose his magic power to control their beliefs.

Slaves will be set free from bondage, people will turn to God as the True Creator, and souls will be saved.

All of this is very likely to happen if enough people

expose the lie and share the truth. That's how God's truths work.

Ephesians 5:11-14 Take no part in the unfruitful works of darkness, but instead expose them. 12 For it is shameful even to speak of the things that they do in secret. 13 But when anything is exposed by the light, it becomes visible, 14 for anything that becomes visible is light. Therefore it says,

"Awake, O sleeper,
and arise from the dead,
and Christ will shine on you."

APPENDIX A: GOD'S WARNINGS
WORSHIPPING FALSE GODS

There are many verses in the Bible that warn us against mythology and worshipping false gods. These are a few.

Romans 1:25 Who changed the truth of God into a lie, and worshipped and served the creature more than the Creator, who is blessed for ever. Amen.

1 Timothy 4:1-2 Now the Spirit expressly says that in later times some will depart from the faith by devoting themselves to deceitful spirits and teachings of demons, 2 through the insincerity of liars whose consciences are seared.

1 Timothy 4:7 Have nothing to do with irreverent, silly myths. Rather train yourself for Godliness.

Romans 1:22-23 Claiming to be wise, they became fools, 23 and exchanged the glory of the immortal God for images resembling mortal man and birds and animals and creeping things.

Ephesians 5:11-12 Take no part in the unfruitful works of darkness, but instead expose them. 12 For it is shameful even to speak of the things that they do in secret.

Leviticus 17:7 So they shall no more sacrifice their sacrifices to goat demons, after whom they whore. This shall be a statute forever for them throughout their generations.

Amos 5:8 He who made the Pleiades and Orion, and turns deep darkness into the morning and darkens the day into night, who calls for the waters of the sea and pours them out on the surface of the Earth, the LORD is his name.

Isaiah 47:9 These two things shall come to you in a moment, in one day; the loss of children and widowhood shall come upon you in full measure, in spite of your many sorceries and the great power of your enchantments.

Isaiah 47:12 Stand fast in your enchantments and your many sorceries, with which you have labored from your youth; perhaps you may be able to succeed; perhaps you may inspire terror.

1 John 4:1-3 Beloved, do not believe every spirit, but test the spirits to see whether they are from God, for many false prophets have gone out into the world. 2 By this you know the Spirit of God: every spirit that confesses that Jesus Christ has come in the flesh is from God, 3 and every spirit that does not confess Jesus is not from God. This is the spirit of the antichrist, which you heard was coming and now is in the world already.

Exodus 20:3-6 You shall have no other gods before me.

Exodus 20:4-6 You shall not make for yourself a carved image, or any likeness of anything that is in heaven above, or that is in the Earth beneath, or that is in the water under the Earth. 5 You shall not bow down to them or serve them, for I the LORD your God am a jealous God, visiting the iniquity of the fathers on the children to the third and the fourth generation of those who hate me, 6 but showing steadfast love to thousands of those who love me and keep my commandments.

Deuteronomy 18:9-14 "When you enter the land which the LORD your God is giving you, you shall not learn to imitate the detestable things of those nations. 10 There shall not be found among you anyone who makes his son or his daughter pass through the fire, one who uses divination, a soothsayer, one who interprets omens, or a sorcerer, 11 or one who casts a spell, or a medium, or a spiritist, or one who consults the dead. 12 For whoever does these things is detestable to the LORD; and because of these detestable things the LORD your God is going to drive them out before you. 13 You are to be blameless before the LORD your God. 14 For these nations, which you are going to dispossess, listen to soothsayers and diviners, but as for you, the LORD your God has not allowed you to do so.

Isaiah 45:5-7 I am the LORD, and there is no other, besides me there is no God; I equip you, though you do not know me, 6 that people may know, from the rising of the sun and from the west, that there is none besides me; I am the LORD, and there is no other. 7 I form light and create darkness; I make well-being and create calamity; I am the LORD, who does all these things.

Matthew 24:24 For false christs and false prophets will

arise and perform great signs and wonders, so as to lead astray, if possible, even the elect.

APPENDIX B: WHAT IS THE FIRMAMENT?
THE BIG SECRET REVEALED IN THE BIBLE

According to the scriptures, the firmament is hard, it holds water back, it stretches well above the earth, and it touches the earth. The stars and the moon are in the firmament, and lastly God's throne sits on top of the firmament. That's a lot to digest, and I want you to see that these statements come directly from the Bible, not from me, and not from any conspiracy theorists. There's no conspiracy here—just the Word of God. What you do with these Biblical truths is up to you, so let's go through them.

The Firmament Separated Solid Water

And God said, Let there be a firmament in the midst of the waters, and let it divide the waters from the waters. 7 And God made the firmament, and divided the waters which were under the firmament from the waters which were above the firmament: and it was so. 8 And God called the firmament Heaven. And the evening and the morning were the second day. Genesis 1:6-8

I want to show you how uncomplicated Bible interpretation can be . There are many times when it helps to know the historical context, which can include secular history or cultural history or religious tradition, and there are times when it can help tremendously to know the Hebrew or Greek, but I want you to see another very important concept in Bible interpretation.

This is actually a part of what theologians would call exegesis. This interpretation, as you will see, includes taking the literal meaning of the words, interpreting consistent with the rest of the Bible, and it does not involve forcing any extraneous world views into the interpretation. It also includes good old fashioned common sense. This is why this is within the rules of good exegetical practice. We'll take this one step at a time, and you'll see how you can do this yourself.

Starting in Genesis 1:6, God created what he called a firmament (from nothing), and he placed it in the midst of the waters. At this point we don't know much about the firmament, except that it is in the midst or middle of "the waters." What is water? We all know what water is, because we drink it, we cook with it, we make coffee with it, we bath in it, we wash our dishes with water, and we water our flowers and plants with water. We also see water when we look across a lake or an ocean. Pretty blue may come to mind, or images of speed boats or sail boats on water may come to mind.

Water is solid. Otherwise we call non-solid forms of water what they are, like steam, moisture, and rain. H_2O comes in three forms or states: liquid, gas, and solid. When it rains on us, we don't say, I'm in the midst of the waters. We say, "It's raining." Depending on how much rain is coming down, we might say, "It's drizzling," or "It's pouring."

When water freezes on the sidewalk, we don't say we are walking on the waters. We say, "it's frozen," or "There's ice on the sidewalk. Be careful."

When your dog is thirsty, you don't say you're going to give him moisture. You say, "Are you thirsty boy? Would you like some water?" And what are we picturing in our minds? Solid water we pour into a bowl.

If you go down to the deep south, like Alabama, in the midst of a hot summer, you're likely to say it is hot and humid. You don't say, "I'm walking in the hot water." If you go into a hot steam bath, you don't say you are in the midst of the waters. You say, "I'm in a hot sauna, and it is really humid in here."

When you are riding in a commercial plane and flying through clouds, do you look out the little window and say, "Oh look, we're flying through the waters." Of course, not. You would get some strange looks. You probably say something like, "We're flying through thick clouds."

So literally the verse says that God created a firmament in water, smack dab in the middle or midst of solid water. At this point, there is no basis from these verses, or anywhere else in the scriptures, that would support the proposition that the firmament was put in anything other than solid water. You can speculate or hypothesize all you want, but you would be outside the literal meaning of the words, and if you are a person who strongly believes in hermeneutics and an exegetical approach to careful Biblical interpretation, you must stick with the Bible and not go off into left field on your own.

As if God didn't make it clear enough that he placed the firmament in solid water, he goes on to say that the firmament is to divide the "waters from the waters." The verse does not say the firmament would divide the clouds, or that it would divide the moisture. It literally says it will divide the waters as though you are slicing water with a dividing wall.

God wanted to emphasize what was actually going to happen, and the way he did that was to restate what was happening by making it abundantly clear that the firmament "divided the waters which were under the firmament from the waters which were above the firmament."

Now you would not talk about dividing the waters which are under something from the waters which are above it, if what you were really referring to was not solid water but mist, or fog, or clouds with moisture. You would only logically and by the plain meaning of the words, say that the firmament divides the waters that are below from the waters that are above when the water you are talking about is solid water.

The Firmament is Solid

Hast thou with him spread out the sky, which is strong, and as a molten looking glass? Job 37:18

In the Hebrew these words mean precisely what they have been translated into in English. Strong means strong, and molten looking glass has the meaning of being hard, like molten glass. While this verse alone would not be conclusive by any means, we study this verse in the context of all these other verses for consistency and logical meaning.

Praise him, ye heavens of heavens, and ye waters that be above the heavens. Psalms 148:4

This verse states that there are waters above the heavens, again alluding to the division of water by the firmament with water being both above and below the firmament. It is a rather curious thing, however, to think of the waters as praising God.

The focus of these verses in Psalms is apparently how God is The Creator of everything, and therefore all of creation praises the creator, even the "waters that be above the heavens." It's not thought by anyone that the creation is animated in praise like a human with a voice, but that the praise is more likely an expression of the fact that God created everything, that everything is sustained by God every moment, and that if God ceased to exist, everything in his creation would cease to exist. God sustains all life, including all of his earthly creation. In that sense, his creation praises him.

This is perhaps not such an unusual thought if one considers the likelihood that the volume of water above the heavens must be so massive, so voluminous, so incredible, that it is worthy of noting how powerful and great the creator must be, the one who not only created all that water, but holds it in place.

If you've ever explored nature on a hike or viewed one of the great wonders of the world, you cannot help but sigh or stand in awe when you first step into the presence of greatness. For example, the first time you see the Grand Canyon, or the first time you stand on the precipice of Niagara Falls are times when you feel a sense of awe. For those of us who are Christians, these are times when we feel the presence of the Almighty Creator, and we stand in praise of him.

Imagine a body of water so massive that it makes the

Grand Canyon or Niagara Falls look like a child's playground! The flood of Noah's time brought so much water, it not only filled the Grand Canyon, it filled every valley on earth and covered every mountain. I think if you and I saw that volume of water, we would stand in awe of God and his creation. We might even suggest that the water itself would praise God.

The heavens declare the glory of God; and the firmament sheweth his handywork. Psalms 19:1

This verse (Psalm 19:1) is a beautiful verse, and there's more theological content here than a casual reading would reveal. First, this verse includes mention of the biggest goal of all creation—to glorify God. What is most important to God? His own glory. There's a famous Westminster Catechism that goes like this:

What is the chief end of man?
Man's chief end is to glorify God and to enjoy him forever.

Throughout the Old Testament and the New Testament you'll see this theme, that God will be glorified. This is an immutable law. God will be glorified. And this verse is reminding us that creation glorifies God and that "the firmament sheweth his handywork."

If the firmament was an invisible curtain of some kind that divided moisture in the clouds, it would be unimpressive and make no sense to say that "the firmament sheweth his handywork." The firmament must be quite impressive to display God's handywork, and anything that declares the glory of God must be incredibly impressive, perhaps gigantic, and must have a huge impact on the earth and God's creation of the earth.

There's a verse that talks about the water from these heavens being released onto the earth, but this is a verse very few people have noticed. It goes unnoticed, because the full context of the verse is not in our heads when we read it, and so we fly right past it. Let me help you with that context.

Have you ever wondered where all the water that flooded the whole earth came from? I'm about to show you, and this doesn't come from me guessing or from me speculating. It comes directly from the Word of God.

In the six hundredth year of Noah's life, in the second month, the seventeenth day of the month, the same day were all the fountains of the great deep broken up, and the windows of heaven were opened. Genesis 7:11

"The windows of heaven were opened" is an extraordinary statement, but most of us have missed the significance of this little phrase our whole lives. We glossed over it because we thought it was just a bit of poetry. There is a lot of poetry in the Psalms and elsewhere, but even that poetry uses words with real meaning. I challenge you to find any verse in the Bible that uses words that mean nothing or have no purpose. All we have to do is remember who the author of the Bible is, and we instantly recall that God doesn't use words with no significance.

Think about the volume of water required to flood the entire earth, fill every valley, and cover the tops of Mount Everest, Mount Denali (formerly Mount McKinley) and every other mountain on the face of the earth. Where would all that water come from? Since we've never had the answer, we typically just blow that question off, and we have said things like, "Well, God can do whatever he wants," or "God brought all the water out of the earth," or "God just made it rain a lot."

There's no question that God has power to do anything, but let's face it, he is the one who created the heavens and the earth, and he is the one who engineered all the laws of physics, geography, climatology, and everything else. Since he had a plan to flood the entire earth, why wouldn't he just do it based on his creation with the existing infrastructure he already had in place? In other words, we don't have to make things up to explain how God did something. Why not just read the scriptures literally and base it on what he told us he created.

Genesis 7:11 says "the windows of heaven were opened" pouring water upon the earth and flooding the entire earth. Most of us assumed the idea of opening "windows of heaven" was poetic, but if we take the verses literally, God opened windows that let the water above the firmament pour onto the earth causing the great flood. It makes more sense than saying that God caused it to rain hard. The volume of water it would take to cover the entire earth would be far beyond what rain could do, and it would take massive quantities of water pouring onto the earth in volumes so large, we cannot comprehend such downpours.

The verse actually stated two causes for all the water that flooded the earth. Besides water pouring through the open windows in the firmament, the fountains of the deep were broken up, so water came from below and above.

Notice that in this interpretation of the scriptures, we don't have to make anything up, like you do with all other theories about the flood. We simply take the Word of God literally, and it says God opened up windows that let the water through, and since he had already explained to us that he created a firmament that was solid and that it separated the waters below (in the oceans) from the waters above the firmament, we don't have to make up any theory. We just take the Bible literally.

The Bible says the waters above the firmament were released upon the earth because God opened the windows in the firmament. Wow! Is that not amazing when you see it in this verse?

In this next verse, we see God poured water "out upon the face of the earth." This would be consistent with water coming from above in large quantities.

It is he that buildeth his stories in the heaven, and hath founded his troop in the earth; he that calleth for the waters of the sea, and poureth them out upon the face of the earth: The Lord is his name. Amos 9:6

The importance to God of the waters that are above is seen in this verse:

Praise him, ye heavens of heavens, and ye waters that be above the heavens. 5 Let them praise the name of the Lord: for he commanded, and they were created. Psalms 148:4-6

When you notice all the praise that is due God throughout the scriptures, and when you read about it in the prayers of the great Believers in the Old Testament and the New Testament, you begin to get a sense of the importance of praising our Creator. He is truly great and awesome and worthy of all our praise and adoration and worship.

Here in Psalms 148 is a reminder again in the words to praise him and "ye waters that be above the heavens, let them praise the name of the Lord." Can you imagine the volume of water that must be "above the heavens" in order for this to even be mentioned as a cause to praise God?

The Sun and Moon In The Firmament

Here's a shocker for you. According to the scriptures the sun and the moon are in the firmament. This is not my interpretation. This is literally what these verses say. Let's look at them closely.

And God made two great lights; the greater light to rule the day, and the lesser light to rule the night: he made the stars also. 17 And God set them in the firmament of the heaven to give light upon the earth. Genesis 1:16-17

I'm aware that theologians might want to debate whether the original Hebrew uses the word "within" or "in" the firmament, and whether that indicates the stars are below the firmament or in a firmament that is not solid. I used the word "within" because it seems apparent that the stars are below the firmament or "within" the earth's side of the firmament. But this is based on all the other verses, and one of the rules of interpretation is the negative—don't strain to interpret a verse in a way that contradicts other verses.

I don't know what you're going to do with the idea that

the sun and the moon are in the firmament (aka "the expanse"). That just blows any Copernican and NASA theories to smithereens, and I'm comfortable leaving that on your coffee table for you to meditate on without saying more.

And I beheld when he had opened the sixth seal, and, lo, there was a great earthquake; and the sun became black as sackcloth of hair, and the moon became as blood; 13 And the stars of heaven fell unto the earth, even as a fig tree casteth her untimely figs, when she is shaken of a mighty wind. Revelation 6:12-13

As if you didn't have verses beating you up on the lack of Biblical support for a heliocentric model of the Universe, Revelation 6:12-13 brings more difficult truths into the picture. At the end when God's judgment is being administered on the earth, this verse states that "the stars of heaven fell unto the earth."

I don't know how someone could turn this verse into an allegory or some sort of poetic expression of the end of the earth. It says the stars will fall to the earth. God didn't say "the meteors fell to earth," or "junk from outer space fell to earth." He literally said the stars will fall to earth.

Since you first fell out of your baby crib, you have been told constantly and by every authority you respect, that the stars are massive and extend billions of light years from the earth. Here's what you've had fed into your brain so many times, it has become part of your brain's neurological network of memories and associations:

Compared to Earth, the Sun is enormous! It contains 99.86% of all of the mass of the entire "solar system". The Sun is 868,400 miles (1,391,000 kilometers) across. This is about 109 times the diameter of Earth. The Sun weighs about 333,000 times as much as Earth. It is so large that about 1,300,000 earths can fit inside of it. Earth is about the size of an average sunspot! [Source: Cool Cosmos]

That's not how the Bible describes the sun. Not even close. Pause to consider the bold statements made in this scientific journal. They somehow claim to know that the sun is 99.86% of all the mass of the entire "solar system"? Really? And how do they know that? And notice how accurate they are. They got it down to not just 99% but 99.86%. Are you serious? Do they really expect us to believe they have any evidence or scientific proof of any of this? Yes, they do expect you to believe it. The more amazing thing is that we, like sheep to the slaughter, believe this nonsense without ever questioning it.

If the Bible is accurate, and I submit it is, then when the prophecy in Revelation is fulfilled and the stars fall to the earth, the sun alone would obliterate the earth because the sun weighs, according to scientists, 333,000 times as much as the earth. But the Bible doesn't say the sun obliterates the earth. On the contrary, the earth survives and has a big future planned by God.

Hmm. If we are to believe God's Word, we are going to have to rethink our Universe, the earth and its relation to the stars.

God's Throne Sits On The Firmament

And above the firmament that was over their heads was the likeness of a throne, as the appearance of a sapphire stone: and upon the likeness of the throne was the likeness as the appearance of a man above upon it. Ezekiel 1:26

This is a description of the firmament above the Angels' heads, and on this firmament is situated the throne of God. In later verses we are told that the "man above upon it" is God. So picture this. We have a solid firmament above us, which separates the water, and on which sits the throne of God. That's an amazing description, wouldn't you agree?

In Isaiah we see another statement that God's throne is situated on this same firmament:

Thus saith the Lord, The heaven is my throne, and the earth is my footstool. Isaiah 66:1

Remember, the firmament is also called heaven, so God's throne is on the heaven or the firmament, and beneath it is the earth.

Where is Heaven Located?

The question of where Heaven is located requires that we understand more about the firmament. The Bible tells us there are three Heavens, and the Apostle Paul affirmed that. One Heaven is the expanse above the earth, or the space we live in and where the birds fly. It is the space above us as we walk the earth.

The second Heaven is the firmament above us and below God's throne. As you'll see below in the verses that describe this firmament, it appears to be a hard substance since it was used by God to actually separate water from water, and to keep the water separated.

The third Heaven is above the firmament (also called the vault) above the earth, and this is where God sits on his throne overlooking the earth. These concepts are repeated in many verses, and here's a verse again reminding us that the firmament is the vault, and a vault is also a hardened substance.

Thick clouds veil him, so that he does not see, and
he walks on the vault of Heaven. Job 22:14

The firmament is just part of the total creation story
that argues vociferously against a heliocentric view of the
Universe and against a spherical earth.

I don't pretend to know things I don't, but this I will
say with great conviction: I believe the Word of God above
all worldly geniuses and scientists. I'll listen to anyone, and
I can learn from anyone, but there is one, and only one, in
whom my trust is absolute, and that one is God Almighty.

APPENDIX C: THE SONS OF GOD

THE MEANING OF "SONS OF GOD" IN GENESIS 6

The Bible cannot be compartmentalized in such a way that you accept some of the scriptures as true and some as untrue. You cannot accept doctrine and the implications of that doctrine in the Old Testament and disregard those implications as played out under the New Covenant.

And you must not dismiss history, even what you perceive as minor history, in the Bible as irrelevant as though it is not connected to the rest of God's story from Genesis through Revelation. There is no story and no verse in the Bible that isn't put there for a reason. Learn to connect the dots. Start putting the whole picture together, and you'll be amazed at what God has been doing.

There's a reason the story of the Nephilim is told in Genesis. They played a major role in the evil deception that filled the world before the flood. Even today we are dealing with the consequences of their wretched history, and when you begin to connect the dots from the Nephilim to God's chosen people and their destiny, your eyes will be opened to much of the deception we are experiencing today.

The confusion for many believers on whether or not the Bible in Genesis 6 actually is referring to fallen angeles from Heaven coming to earth to mate with women surrounds the phrase *"sons of God"* in Genesis 6. Many believers do not believe the Bible actually states that there were fallen angels who mated with women to create "Nephilim" or hybrids on earth, because they believe that "sons of God" is referring to men, not fallen angels.

Because it makes all the difference in the world whether "Sons of Gods" are men on earth or fallen angels from Heaven, I have included this careful biblical analysis that I think you'll agree persuasively demonstrates that the phrase definitely refers to fallen angels, and therefore the Bible clearly states that fallen angeles procreated with women on earth.

Once you see how many verses in the Bible affirm that, you'll be able to move past that issue and focus on issues related to flat earth and how on the earth anyone, like you and me, could have been so thoroughly fooled into believing anything but the true Genesis account of creation.

Satan and his proxies have continuously tried to get you and me to believe there is no God, that man alone is the authority on earth, and a big part of Satan's strategy is to get you to think the earth is something totally different than what God created. Mass deception, and the explanation of that mass deception is detailed in the chapter on the Babylonian System.

If you have any issue or confusion regarding fallen angels procreating with women on earth, please read this Appendix in full, and I think you'll see the biblical basis is actually affirmed by the Bible itself.

Who Were The Sons of God?

There are two primary positions on who the Sons of God were. One argues that they were men from the line of Seth and they mated with women from the line of Cain. The line of Cain and Ham has many evil people later and giants in the Land of Canaan who were evil. The line of Seth is considered the purer line that ultimately led to Jesus.

The other argument is that the Sons of God were angels, and in the context of Genesis 6 they were fallen angels who came to earth from Heaven to mate with women.

One of the best ways to interpret a verse in the Bible is to let other verses in the Bible do that for you. Let's look more closely at the use of the phrase "Sons of God" in the Bible. We don't need to use any other extra biblical sources or apocrypha to do this.

The Sons of God show up in Job 1:6 and are clearly appearing before God in Heaven and alongside Satan. This verse leads us to believe the Sons of God are angels in God's presence. Obviously, men from earth do not show up in Heaven to talk with God and with Satan by their side.

Now there was a day when the sons of God came to present themselves before the LORD, and Satan also came among them. Job 1:6 and Job 2:1

And there is this extraordinary response by God to Job:

"Where were you when I laid the foundation of
  the earth?
Tell me, if you have understanding.
Who determined its measurements—surely you
  know!
Or who stretched the line upon it?
On what were its bases sunk,
or who laid its cornerstone,
when the morning stars sang together
and all the sons of God shouted for joy?" Job 38:4-7

We have God Himself referring to "sons of God" in Heaven who clearly are angels, not men.

The conservative Dr. John MacArthur persuasively argues that "Sons of Gods" were angels, and he interprets Genesis 6 to mean fallen angels did come to earth and procreate with women.

Some have argued that the sons of God were the sons of Seth who cohabited with the daughters of Cain; others suggest they were perhaps human kings wanting to build harems. But the passage puts strong emphasis on the angelic vs. human contrast. The NT places this account in sequence with other Genesis events and identifies it as involving fallen angels who indwelt men (see notes on 2Pe 2:4, 5; Jude 6). Matthew 22:30 does not necessarily negate the possibility that angels are capable of procreation, but just that they do not marry. To procreate physically, they had to possess human, male bodies. (MacArthur Study Bible Notes NIV) [Underscore added]

In the Preaching the Word Commentary Series, the analysis shows the Sons of God are angels:

Therefore, understanding that "the sons of God" are angels (here in Genesis 6, fallen angels) . . . what we must have here in "the sons of God" marrying "the daughters of man" is fallen angels (demons) commandeering the souls of men (demon-possession, in modern parlance), and these demonized men marrying the daughters of other men. It is these same angelic lowlifes whom Peter and Jude reference as having been imprisoned at the time of

197

the flood and as now being kept in dungeons for ultimate judgment. Unbelievable? I think not. As the highly respected Old Testament scholar Gordon Wenham has said, "If the modern reader finds this story incredible, that reflects a materialism that tends to doubt the existence of spirits, good or ill. But those who believe that the creator could unite himself to human nature in the Virgin's womb will not find this story intrinsically beyond belief." (Preaching the Word Commentary Series (41 Vols.) - PTW)

Some have read the Septuagint (LXX) and interpreted the Genesis 6 verses to mean men on earth were not angels, but that doesn't square with the literal translation of the verses:

---

1. And it came to pass when men began to be numerous upon the earth, and daughters were born to them, 2. that the *sons of God having seen the daughters of men that they were beautiful, took to themselves wives of all whom they chose. 3. And the Lord God said, My Spirit shall certainly not remain among these men for ever, because they are flesh, but their days shall be an hundred and twenty years. 4. Now the giants were upon the earth in those days; and after that when the sons

of God were wont to go in to the daughters of men, they bore children to them, those were the giants of old, the men of renown. Gen 6:1-4, Philadelphus, Ptolemy; Philadelphus, Ptolemy. Septuagint - the Complete Old Testament book containing Apocrypha and additional books directly translated from the Hebrew Bible (p. 13). Kindle Edition.

The asterisk in front of "sons of God" is in the original 1844 translation of the Greek Septuagint, known as the Lancelot Brenton translation (available on Amazon and entitled "Septuagint Complete, Old Testament Book With Aprocypha by Lancelot Breenton"), and at the bottom of the page the asterisk by Genesis 6:2 indicates that "angels of God" was also a Septuagint translation in one of the three Septuagint versions. You can see that "angels of God" translation in the Septuagint version entitled "The Lexham English Septuagint" and I've linked this to Amazon.

So it is clear that the translator of at least one version of the Septuagint translated the original Greek to mean that fallen angels did come down to earth and procreate with women. This is understandable because of the clear evidence throughout other Bible verses that there were fallen angels, that they were identified with the giants, aka the Nephilim, and that these are cursed by God for their sin by being chained deep within the earth until God releases them at the end for judgment.

I love what Kent Hughes says in his commentary on this subject, and note the New Testament references to the fallen angels, their connection with the flood and their curse by God:

I was made aware of the New Testament passages that link fallen angels and the flood. For example, 1 Peter 3:19, 20 alludes to Christ preaching upon his death "to the spirits in prison, because they formerly did not obey, when God's patience waited in the days of Noah, while the ark was being prepared, in which a few, that is, eight persons, were brought safely through water." The word for "spirits" (pneumata) is used in the Bible only to describe supernatural beings - here the fallen angels of Genesis 6. And 2 Peter 2:4-5, 9 references the same fallen angels in the context of the flood, as Peter warns that God will also hold the unrighteous for judgment:

For if God did not spare angels when they sinned, but cast them into hell and committed them to chains of gloomy darkness to be kept until the judgment; if he did not spare the ancient world, but preserved Noah, a herald of righteousness, with seven others . . . then the Lord knows how to rescue the godly from trials, and to keep the unrighteous under punishment until the day of judgment.

Similarly Jude 6 references these same angels:

"And the angels who did not stay within their own position of authority, but left their proper dwelling, he has kept in eternal chains under gloomy darkness until the judgment of the great day."

In addition to these New Testament references, I have learned that the angel interpretation of Genesis 6 is the oldest view. The earliest Jewish exegetes held this view as represented in such sources as 1 Enoch, the Book of Jubilees, the Septuagint (LXX), the writings of Philo and Josephus, and the Dead Sea Scrolls. The same position was held by the early Christian writers Clement of Alexandria, Tertullian, and Origen. (Preaching the Word Commentary Series (41 Vols.) - PTW)

In verse 4 the "giants were upon the earth," which is understood by theologians today as meaning the offspring of the fallen angels also known throughout scripture as Nephilim. Various Bible translations use "giants" or "Nephilim" in Genesis 6.

One last definitive proof I'll mention about the use of the phrase "sons of God" in the Old Testament is that every time it is used in the OT, it is the Hebrew phrase "bene ha elohim." There are only five uses of this phrase in the Hebrew Bible. It is used is Gen 6:2, Gen 6:4, Job 1:6, Job 2:1, and Job 38:4 and 38:6-7. When you read all of these verses, it becomes clear that the same meaning of "bene ha elohim" is used in Genesis 6. Sons of God were angels, not men on earth. [See an excellent video on this entitled "Who are the Sons of God in Genesis 6?" by Doug Petrovich.

What About "Sons of God" in The New Testament?

In the Old Testament "Sons of God" always refer to angels, but in the New Testament "Sons of God" always refers to those who are godly and whose inheritance makes them members of the family of God, in other words sons of God. This has confused some people.

In the OT "Sons of God" always refer to those who were born or created directly by God himself. God created angels Himself, so they are directly "Sons of God".

In the NT believers are adopted as sons into the Kingdom by faith in Jesus Christ as their savior, which is to say that humans who become believers had an earthly father unlike the angels whose father creator was God Himself. Believers only become "Sons of God" when we become believers through Christ and are adopted into God's family so that he becomes our father and we become sons.

Here are all the OT and NT uses of "Sons of God" shown on this image:

Address	Verse	Context	Meaning
Gen. 6:2	"that the sons of God saw that the daughters of men were beautiful; and they took wives for themselves, whomever they chose."	Nephilim, the wickedness of man. SOG took wives of women	Angels
Gen. 6:4	"The Nephilim were on the earth in those days, and also afterward, when the sons of God came in to the daughters of men, and they bore children to them."	Nephilim, the wickedness of man. SOG took wives of women	Angels
Job 1:6	"Now there was a day when the sons of God came to present themselves before the LORD, and Satan also came among them."	SOG could be the good angels and/or bad angels	Angels
Job 2:1	"Again there was a day when the sons of God came to present themselves before the LORD, and Satan also came among them to present himself before the LORD."	SOG could be the good angels and/or bad angels	Angels
Job 38:7	"And all the sons of God shouted for joy?"	SOG good angels	Angels
Matt. 5:9	"Blessed are the peacemakers, for they shall be called sons of God."	SOG is those who a godly, trust in God	People
Luke 20:36	"for they cannot even die anymore, because they are like angels, and are sons of God, being sons of the resurrection."	SOG is those who a godly, trust in God	People
Rom. 8:14	"For all who are being led by the Spirit of God, these are sons of God."	SOG is those who a godly, trust in God	People
Rom. 8:19	"For the anxious longing of the creation waits eagerly for the revealing of the sons of God."	SOG is those who a godly, trust in God	People
Gal. 3:26	"For you are all sons of God through faith in Christ Jesus."	SOG is those who a godly, trust in God	People

This beautiful summary was created by Matt Slick. The link on the image goes to his website.

Some have argued that angels cannot have sex, and have dismissed the Genesis 6 account summarily. The Bible does tell us that angels don't marry, but it never says angels cannot procreate.

For in the resurrection they neither marry, nor are given in marriage, but are as the angels of God in heaven. Matthew 22:30

It would seem angels can have sex, and they can take human form. There are many verses that indicate angels have appeared as humans, and don't forget that we have been told we may unknowingly entertain angels.

Remember what happened at Lot's house in Sodom? A crowd of men pounded on the door demanding that Lot give them the two angels who were in Lot's house so they could have sex with them. These two angels took the form of men, and that apparently included the whole human body and its ability to have sex.

Before they had gone to bed, all the men from every part of the city of Sodom —both young and old— surrounded the house. They called to Lot, "Where are the men who came to you tonight? Bring them out to us so that we can have sex with them." Genesis 19:4-5

More proof that fallen angels actually had sex with women on earth, which a lot of people just have a hard time believing, is found in the New Testament in Jude:

And the angels who did not keep their proper domain, but left their own abode, He has reserved in everlasting chains under darkness for the judgment of the great day; as Sodom and Gomorrah, and the cities around them in a similar manner to these, having given themselves over to sexual immorality and gone after strange flesh, are set forth as an example, suffering the vengeance of eternal fire. Jude 1:6-7 (Orthodox Study Bible Text—The Septuagint)

And other versions also make it clear that the reference to sexual immorality in Sodom and Gomorrah is compared to the sexual sins of the fallen angels. This is the context and the grammatical connection recognized by all common versions of the Bible, including the ESV, too:

And the angels who did not stay within their own position of authority, but left their proper dwelling, he has kept in eternal chains under gloomy darkness until the judgment of the great day— just as Sodom and Gomorrah and the surrounding cities, which likewise indulged in sexual immorality and pursued unnatural desire, serve as an example by undergoing a punishment of eternal fire. Jude 1:6-7

The Bible also gives us extensive lists of genealogies, which clearly show the lines to the giants who are described in multiple verses in the Old Testament, and who are also identified as evil. All of these giants trace their origin to Genesis 6 and the fallen angels.

Conclusion: The "Sons of God" in Genesis 6 are fallen angels, and fallen angels came down from Heaven and procreated with women.

APPENDIX D: THE DECEPTION OF THE ROMAN CATHOLIC CHURCH
ALL CHRISTIANS NEED TO KNOW THIS

The Roman Catholic Church has played such a significant role for Satan's cause going all the way back to the first pope in the 6th century A.D., I'm including the best documentary I have found on this subject. [You have to have an Internet connection.]

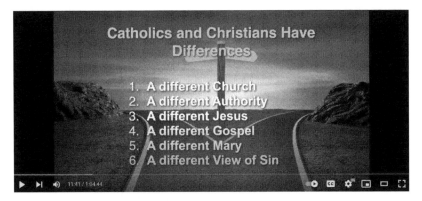

On a computer type bit.ly/3FQI2KW in your browser, or search for "Ex-Catholic Exposes the TWISTED Teachings of the Catholic Church | Mike Gendron"

This video ought to be mandatory for every christian, because far too many believe that the Roman Catholic Church is a christian church and that they believe essentially the same doctrines Protestants believe. The massive deception at the Vatican for centuries is shocking. But do not miss the fact that they tried to keep God's Word from us.

One more excellent and shorter video I recommend is by Dr. John Barnett entitled "How Satan Uses Paganism in Roman Catholicism."

APPENDIX E:
HELIOSORCERY
A VIDEO DOCUMENTARY OF THE SORCERY
OF HELIOCENTRISM

You must have an Internet connection to view this video.

On a computer type bit.ly/3ZvjKgV in your browser, or search for
**"Heliosorcery (2022) | Exposing the Occult Origins of
Heliocentrism | Full Documentary"**

ALSO BY
CASPIAN "CASPER" SARGINSON, J.D.
THE EASY WAY TO SEE ALL OF THE
AUTHOR'S BOOKS IN ALL VERSIONS

See all of Casper Sarginson's books on Amazon by touching this QR code if you're on a smart device, or by scanning this code with another smart device, or simply type the URL below into a browser.

In a browser type https://bit.ly/3ZTcBrN

Made in United States
Orlando, FL
31 August 2024

50992391R30122